Answering the Creative Call Workbook

Also by Kim Antieau:

Old Mermaids Books
The Blue Tail
Church of the Old Mermaids
The First Book of Old Mermaids Tales
The Fish Wife
An Old Mermaid Journal
The Old Mermaids Book of Days and Nights
The Old Mermaids Book of Days and Nights: A Year and a Day Journal
The Old Mermaids Oracle

Novels
Broken Moon
Butch
Coyote Cowgirl
Deathmark
The Desert Siren
The Gaia Websters
Her Frozen Wild
Jewelweed Station
The Jigsaw Woman
Maternal Instincts
Mercy, Unbound
The Monster's Daughter
Queendom: Feast of the Saints
The Rift
Ruby's Imagine
Swans in Winter
Whackadoodle Times
Whackadoodle Times Two

Nonfiction
Answering the Creative Call
Certified
Counting on Wildflowers
The Salmon Mysteries
The Salmon Mysteries Workbook
Under the Tucson Moon

Short Story Collections
Entangled Realities (with Mario Milosevic)
Haunted
Tales Fabulous and Fairy
Trudging to Eden

Cartoons
Fun With Vic and Jane

Photography
www.kimantieau.smugmug.com

Also by Mario Milosevic:

Novels
Claypot Dreamstance
The Coma Monologues
The Doctor and The Clown
Kyle's War
The Last Giant
Splitting
Terrastina and Mazolli

Short Story Collections
15 Strange Tales of Crime and Mystery
Entangled Realities (with Kim Antieau)
Labor Days
Miniatures

Poetry
Animal Life
Fantasy Life
Love Life

Answering the Creative Call Workbook

Kim Antieau

Answering the Creative Call Workbook
by Kim Antieau

Copyright © 2018 by Kim Antieau

http://www.kimantieau.com

ISBN: 978-1-949644-02-9

All rights reserved.

No part of this book may be reproduced
without written permission of the author.

Cover illustration, *Barefoot Moon* copyright © Nancy Norman

Special thanks to Nancy Milosevic.

Published by Green Snake Publishing
www.greensnakepublishing.com

This is for my readers
who ask me how it's done.

Now you know . . . and
now you can do it too.

Contents

Introduction 9

Begin to Begin 13
Preparation 20
Know Thyself 30
Money 40
Crafty Art 44
Answering the Call, Part I 50
Answering the Call, Part II 56
Speaking of Insanity: Addictions 62
Time 68
When and Where 74
Creative Space 78
Centering 82
Perspective 90
Creative Cycles 98
Dreams 106
Getting Physical 114
Nature and The Invisibles 118
Creation Stories 126
Practice 138
Journaling 139
Visual Arts 144
Fiction 152
Creative Nonfiction 161
Poetry (*by Mario Milosevic*) 172
Be Full of Yourself 181

About the Author 182

Introduction

All writing advice is memoir.
Mario Milosevic

A FEW WORDS first. . . .

We are born creative. You will hear me say this again and again. Within these pages you will find ideas on how to jump-start your natural creativity. But the best advice I've ever heard or given about writing is, "Just do it." Just sit down and do it.

See. There you have it. You don't need to buy the book after all.

Maybe you need a bit of inspiration before you just do it? Or maybe you want some exercises to get yourself into shape before you jump into the imaginal realms? You'll find all of that here. At least that is my hope.

Don't let this book or anything I say in it stop you from writing, painting, composing, or creating any other kind of art. My purpose is to get you started and to keep you going.

I am primarily a novel writer. That is what I do and know best, but I also take photos, work with clay, and draw a bit. For those of you who are visual or musical artists, please adapt my creativity tips to fit your medium. Or try them first as writing exercises and see what happens. Each of you is the artist, the

> My purpose is to get you started and to keep you going.

> Don't worry about being the best or the most original.

creator, the storyteller. You get to decide what works for you.

As I said, the best writing advice, the best art advice, the best creative advice is this: Just do it. Don't worry about being perfect. Don't worry about being the best or the most original. And certainly don't worry about being the most famous or the richest. Creativity is a natural part of your being that you've possessed since you were born. This book is about helping you get out of your way and letting those creations flow easily from you.

Mostly, my hope is that this book gives you permission to be creative in your own way.

The workbook has all the text from the original and a bit more. We've set up the workbook with extra pages—lined and unlined—so that you can journal about your process with words and/or with drawings, paintings, collages. We've also left wide margins so you can take notes or draw in them. Make this entire book your art piece.

Creativity Tip

This first tip is one of the most important.

All criticism is opinion, no matter how right the person thinks he/she is. Although we all need to learn our craft, whatever it is, after a while, we have to make the work our own. Novel writing isn't done by committee. Quit asking for other people's opinion because that's all you'll get: opinion. And that really doesn't mean much.

Journal Page:

Begin to Begin

*Begin with the stirring,
begin with the stirring
in your own dark center,
begin. . . .*
Gwendolyn Endicott

AH, HERE WE are on this journey together. Some might call it a pilgrimage. We're wandering, sauntering, on a walkabout to discover or reinvigorate our creativity.

It's important to begin this journey with a beginner's mind, especially when we think we know all there is to know.

Zen Buddhist teacher Shunryu Suzuki said, "In the beginner's mind there are many possibilities, in the expert's mind there are few."

For now, while reading and doing the exercises in this book, think of yourself as a beginner: a beginner with enthusiasm, eagerness, and openness. Even if you don't feel any of this yet, I encourage you to pretend you do: Fake it until you make it.

The word enthusiasm comes from the Greek word "enthous" which means to be "possessed by a god, inspired." Although you may not feel particularly inspired by anything yet, I'm betting you will feel enthusiasm by the end of this book. And it can

Begin with a beginner's mind.

Let go of your notions of perfection.

be *your* kind of enthusiasm. That's the important thing to remember about all of this. Your creativity is your creativity. If you are a bubbly kind of person, be a bubbly kind of person with your creations. Or not. If you're more introverted, be introverted. Or not. Your "possession by a god" will look different from anyone else's. That leads us back to the next thing. Begin with a beginner's mind, even if you feel like you're an expert about creativity, even if you feel like you're an expert on yourself and you swear you're not creative.

I will say this again and again: Let go of your notions of perfection.

Yep. This will help you achieve a beginner's mind, and it will also help your stress level while being creative. Being creative is not about you writing the great American novel, although you may do that. This is not about you painting the greatest picture since Vincent Van Gogh created *The Starry Night,* although you may do that. It's about tapping into that glorious creative part of your being. Ideas of perfection don't belong.

So let go of your notions of perfection unless you have in mind the original Old French definition of perfection which means "to complete." Then yes, by all means, achieve perfection by finishing whatever you are creating: a novel, poem, photograph, quilt, painting, musical composition.

Recently a friend of ours returned a book to the library where my husband Mario works. It doesn't matter which book. It was a popular book, and millions of people had bought copies of it and read it. This friend—an artist who has been unable to finish anything for several years now—said to Mario, "I don't understand why people liked this book. It really needed some editing. She repeated herself. It is a deeply flawed book."

Mario said, "Did it occur to you that maybe it was popular for exactly those reasons? Good stories are organic. They're not about having every word in place, every punctuation mark perfect, and all the gnarly bits smoothed out."

This artist had not been able to work successfully for years because he saw each of his creations as imperfect, and he couldn't figure out how to make them perfect. So all of his works remained unfinished.

Yikes!

I know people who have been working on the same novel for years. They're trying to perfect it, get every word right. There may be a place for novels like that, but they are not novels I want to read. Fiction is about storytelling. A good oral storyteller does not necessarily have every word "right." She tells the story as though she is talking to a friend, even if that friend is a large audience. Yes, she has skills; she has practiced and probably rehearsed, but she also understands that the flavor, the rhythm, even the words will change depending upon the audience and the characters in the story.

Writing down a story requires the same skills and the same ability to let go. You don't want people thinking about your great sentence construction or your stunning imagery. You want to create a world that your reader can easily step into. You are the guide; you are not the star. Novel writing isn't about you: It's about the reader; it's about the story.

Remember the last time you listened to someone tell a good story. At the end of it, you probably thought, "What a great story!" You were not thinking, "What a great sentence." That's the best reaction a novel writer can get, too. Your words become an incantation, drawing the reader into the story so that it becomes her story. You as the writer don't want to do anything to break that spell. Those nondescript guides on fantastical journeys are often actually great sorcerers, witches, and magicians in disguise. They are able to do their magic without bringing undue attention to themselves.

> Don't worry about getting every word right. Get the story right.

So let notions of perfection fly out the window. Tell a good story. Don't worry about getting every word right. Get the entire story right. It's not piecemeal. It's the whole meal.

I'm not telling you to do shoddy work. I'm suggesting that you not obsess. I'm suggesting you let go and let the story flow.

You'll soon see that the heart of good storytelling is not perfection or the quest for it. The heart of good storytelling is magic.

And the other thing: Just do it. Finish it. Move on. And if you can't finish it, put it away and move on. Start, finish, move on. That is the best thing you can do for your creative flow.

Don't let anyone decide whether what you are creating is worthwhile or not. No one else gets to make that call. Ever. Not an art gallery owner, a publisher, a family member, or a friend.

This is so important to get.

If your worth is tied up in someone else deciding the worth of your creations, untie it. Now.

> Perfectionism can stifle creativity.

You are a creative being, whether you acknowledge it or not. For the time being, no one is allowed to judge your creations: not even you.

Do the creativity tips. Or don't. Let yourself contemplate your creativity, beauty, creation. Let yourself walk in beauty, dance in beauty, play in beauty. Beauty is defined here as creation: whatever you create. It can be a meal you make, a pant leg you hem, a story you tell your children, or any of the exercises you do in this book.

I had a friend who was an artist and a teacher. She had a right and wrong way to do absolutely everything. This began to weigh heavily on her and the people around her, particularly in the last months of her life. She would walk into a room and immediately see that the art was hanging on the walls wrong, the color of the paint was wrong, the way the furniture was arranged was wrong.

One day she told me there was a correct way and a wrong way to pass a bowl of potatoes around the table. I said, "What if in another country or in another family, they considered it correct to pass around the bowl in the opposite direction. Would they be wrong?" "Yes," she said. She was a brilliant woman, but after a while, her notions of what was right and wrong in art bled into everything in her life.

Perfectionism can stifle creativity. Instead of enjoying the creative process, you will forever be comparing your creations to other people's work. This might prevent you from ever thinking your work is good enough.

Remember: An opinion on whether a painting, story, or sculpture is good or bad is not a fact. It is not a truth. It is a subjective opinion.

At least for now, let go of your notions of perfection, and embrace the beginner's mind.

Creativity Tip

Just do it.

Begin. Stop making excuses. Stop saying, "I'll start once this, that, or the other thing happens." You don't have to know everything. Perfection isn't required. Sit down at the computer, get a pad of paper, or use this workbook and begin writing. Get your pencils, watercolors, or oils or get out your drawing pad and begin. Whatever it is. Start it. And then keep going. And then finish it. Begin. Keep going. Finish it. Begin again on something else. Keep going. Finish it. Move on. Begin again. Keep going. Finish it.

> Don't let anyone decide whether what you are creating is worthwhile or not.

Journal Page:

Preparation

We thirst at first.
Emily Dickinson

YOU WERE BORN creative. Everyone is.

You don't believe me? Try to remember when you were a child with a box of crayons and a coloring book. I bet you colored outside the lines until someone directed your little hand back inside the picture, telling you the "right" way to do it.

You weren't doing it the wrong way. You were being creative. (OK, maybe you were also working on developing your motor skills.)

But, you say, there are right and wrong ways to color. To draw. To write.

Who says?

If you were raised in the Western culture as I was, you were not encouraged to be creative—unless you were creative within certain boundaries, like staying inside the lines on a coloring page, mixing together only those paint colors that were pleasing to the teacher, or telling only those stories that did not question the status quo or upset anyone, especially family or teachers.

I bet you doodled when you were a child. Until someone pointed out your drawings weren't very realistic.

> Maybe now you feel like something is lacking in your life.

Or perhaps you wore clothes that were not in fashion.

Or maybe you thought about coloring outside the lines, mixing paint colors until you came up with black, wearing bizarre clothes, or drawing exaggerated figures.

You can't remember?

That's all right. Trust me on this one thing: You are creative.

This book will help you remember how to color outside the lines.

Maybe you are someone who knows you are creative. People have been telling you that since you were a child. "She's got such a vivid imagination." "He's a creative kid." "She's always thinking up something." Yet most of the time when someone mentioned you might be creative or have a vivid imagination, it never felt like a compliment. "I wish she'd be a doctor, but she's one of those creative types."

Everyone knew you were creative, including you, but you followed another path anyway, because you saw very clearly at an early age that true creativity, especially originality, is seldom rewarded in our culture. And you wanted to have a prosperous life or a normal life or you didn't want to rock the boat, so you put away your crayons, paints, notebooks full of drawings or words, and got a real job.

Maybe now you feel like something is lacking in your life. In your being. And you want to find out what you've missed.

Or maybe you are one of the creative people who followed your intuition, followed your creative path, and you're tired, without any money or property to speak of, wondering why you took this path in the first place. In fact, you're so tired of trying to make your mark in this world doing the thing you do best that you're ready to give up.

Don't.

Perhaps within these pages, you can find succor,

> Trust me on this one thing: You are creative.

joy, inspiration, and renewed creativity as you learn to color outside the lines once again.

CREATIVITY TIP

Use the coloring sheets on the following pages or get several copies of a coloring page you like off the internet. You'll also need a box of crayons.

Color your coloring page. And go outside the lines. It doesn't have to look like anything you've ever done before. It can look like a second grader did it. Just color. You don't even have to think about the colors. Close your eyes and pick a crayon. You can darken in the entire page if you want. Let yourself go. Don't judge what you're doing. If you feel tense, breathe and color.

Now take another copy of the same coloring sheet and do it again. This time be a little more choosy about what colors you use. Pick colors you especially like. Make sure you color outside the lines. But this time, go outside the lines to create a particular effect, perhaps, instead of coloring to color, like you did last time.

Keep encouraging yourself

Keep doing this until you start having fun—or until you run out of copies. When you're finished, turn over one of the sheets of paper and use a black pen or black crayon and make your own quick sketch of a flower, house, bird, fork, whatever. Then color in this drawing, going outside the lines. Make another similar drawing, but this time when you color, stay within the lines.

Now look at them all. Which coloring sheet or drawing do you like best? As you decide this, let go of any notions of perfection. Which drawing was more fun to do? Which drawing or coloring sheet looks more creative? Which expresses more about you?

Choose one of these coloring pages that you like and tape, pin, or hang it up somewhere where you can see it daily. When you look at it, remind yourself that sometimes it is good to go outside the lines.

If this exercise is stressful for you, keep doing it over the next few days. Keep encouraging yourself as you do it.

Journal Page:

Know Thyself

Know thyself.
Pythia, Delphi oracle

LET ME TELL you a bit about my creative process. I started telling stories by drawing pictures when I was very young, before kindergarten. In the first grade, I won first place for a drawing I made of the cowboy in the moon. I was quite proud, but I remember deciding then and there that being an artist was not the way to go: I couldn't make a living drawing pictures, so I had better stick to telling stories—via writing. I put my pencils and crayons away and didn't pick them up until a few decades later.

I don't know where I came up with the idea that writers could make money and artists couldn't. My father was a teacher, and my mother stayed at home taking care of five children. We always had books and art in our house. The art wasn't original. We had copies of famous art on our walls, but still, I got to walk past a Mary Cassatt painting nearly every day of my life. My parents never pushed us to think about a career and certainly not when I was five or six years old. They didn't talk about money problems around us; in fact my father told me the bills were none of my business.

So why did I think I couldn't make a living as

an artist? And more importantly, why did I care so much about this that I made a conscious decision to become a writer rather than an artist when I was in the first grade?

I don't really know. My mother grew up during the Great Depression, and she remembered it vividly. Whenever we asked her what she wanted for her birthday or Christmas, she would say, "Money." She had experienced such poverty and uncertainty as a child, and she was scarred by it.

My father was a few years younger than my mother, and he didn't remember the Depression. I don't think the Depression hit my father's family as hard as it did my mother's. My father lived on a farm, and my grandfather Antieau had a job off the farm, too.

My mother's father died before she was a teen, so her family lost the major wage-earner in the household when she was quite young. My mother had to quit school and get a job to help support the family. So even though my parents encouraged us to be whoever we wanted to be, I understood the ramifications of poverty early on.

When I learned to write, I began scribbling stories in pencil on any paper I could find. My teachers and parents encouraged me. My mother told me I should write in pen because when I was older and famous, people would want to see the work I had done as a child—and pencil fades. So I stopped using a pencil and carefully wrote in pen over the stories I had already written in pencil. I still have the first long story I wrote when I was a little girl. It is called "Lily Goes to Fairyland," and it is illustrated with stick drawings. (Apparently I had not yet given up drawing completely.)

As a child, I spent most of my waking hours out of doors. Even when I was writing, I often sat under the tall old oaks in our yard. I interacted with Na-

> I interacted with Nature, passing afternoons stretched out on soft beds of moss, staring up at the clouds.

ture, passing afternoons stretched out on soft beds of moss, staring up at the clouds.

I was Nature's child: I knew which bird songs came from which kind of bird, which leaf came from which kind of tree, and what the air smelled like before snow or rain. I watched a family of mice grow up in a rotted log, recognized the sound of a rattler in the grass, and never got lost in the woods. I climbed trees and sat in them for hours, singing songs I made up. I was a country girl, a wild child, through and through.

I wanted to learn to play piano, or some other instrument, but back then they tested kids for "musical ability." They told my parents I didn't have any musical potential, so they shouldn't waste their money buying me an instrument. I had always been a good student in every subject, so it was a shock to my little self. After that diagnosis, I never tried singing or playing an instrument.

I wrote all kinds of stories when I was in elementary school. During my high school years, I wrote a novel a year, usually during the summer months. I wrote them out on lined paper and then bound each one into a book.

In college, I worked on the school newspaper and the literary magazine, eventually becoming literary editor and then editor-in-chief of the magazine. I continued to write stories. For one of my writing classes, I wrote a science fiction story. The professor scribbled on my paper, "If you *must* write this sort of thing, I suppose this story accomplished what you wanted it to." Or something like that. After that assessment, I went back to writing mainstream *New Yorker*-like stories without a plot in sight.

For my last class for my Master of Arts degree, I attended Clarion Science Fiction and Fantasy Writers' Workshop. This was a six-week summer workshop where I lived in a dorm in East Lansing, Michigan with 18 other writers. We were treated to a different writer-in-residence each week. It was the first time in my life I was surrounded by people like myself. They were quirky, opinionated, talented, creative, annoying, and amazing. I loved every minute of it. Our instructors were Robin Scott Wilson, Algis Budrys, Avram Davidson, Kit Reed, Kate Wilhelm, and Damon Knight. I met Canadian writer Mario Milosevic at this workshop. A year later, we married and then moved to the coast of Oregon to begin our lives together as writers.

Clarion was wonderful. I found my true love, and I was encouraged to keep on writing. I learned that a writer was someone who wrote, not someone who talked about wanting to be a writer.

I never doubted my ability to be creative, until I got sick. Less than a year after moving to the coast, I began experiencing a number of health problems. I was unable to read and write for nearly a year. I got better, and then worse, and then better. Sometimes I could write, sometimes I couldn't.

My mode of creativity was writing, but I was having trouble writing. I had a choice. Was I going to spend my life on the couch, sick, unable to write most of the time, or was I going to see if I could be creative in other ways?

I decided to start a garden. Doing this saved my life. On days when I was too exhausted or dizzy to do almost anything, I was able to sit on the dirt and slowly pull up weeds. For me, having a vegetable garden was the ultimate creative act.

After that, I made pretty pouches and filled them with herbs. I started cooking. I got butcher paper and drew and drew and drew and drew. Sometimes I drew black lines over and over again. I started drawing my comic strip *Vic & Jane*. I published and edited a fiction magazine.

After a spring flood one year, I walked to the Columbia River and snagged some long sticks, took them back to the house, sanded them, decorated them

> Having a vegetable garden was the ultimate creative act.

with stones and feathers, and called them walking sticks. I made candles. I molded sculptures. Took photographs. Spent hours drawing my feet. Or my belly. My hands. I threw great parties. I danced. I put on an art show at my house.

Writing had become my sole identity. When I experienced difficulty writing, I had to realize I could be a whole person whether I wrote or not: I could be creative in many ways. I didn't have to be the best at whatever it was, I didn't have to do it perfectly, and I could have fun with it.

Creativity Tip

Be kind to yourself. Become aware of how you talk to yourself. You are with you all the time, so what you say to yourself is more important than what anyone else says. If you really listen to your self talk, you'll find you are often repeating what someone said to you once upon a time.

When I was a teenager with a face full of pimples, my mother told me to look in the mirror every morning and tell myself I was beautiful. "Because you can't count on anyone else telling you," she said. She was right. I looked in the mirror and told myself I was beautiful. I didn't think I was ugly, didn't act like I was ugly, and eventually my face cleared up.

So what do you say to yourself about your creativity?

Do you say: *I can't draw. I can't paint. I can't write. This is stupid; no one will buy it. I have a lousy voice. I'm ugly.*

Or do you say things like: *I'm a great writer. I'm the best damn soprano west of the Mississippi. I am beautiful.*

If you're saying crappy things to yourself, you need to stop it. Most of us are habitually cruel to ourselves, continuing to indoctrinate ourselves in the ways of the anti-creative society we live in. Be aware if you're being disrespectful to yourself. If you're hearing in your head, "Gawd, you're so stupid," for instance, change it and say to yourself, "I'm sorry, I'm not stupid. I'm very smart. Smart enough to stop saying bad things about myself."

I realize this might sound silly to you. I'm not big into affirmations as a way of life. However, words are powerful, and they do affect how we feel about ourselves.

Now, write down those nasty and positive things you say to yourself. Look at your list and figure out ways you can change those nasties. "I am not creative!" becomes, "Yes, I am very creative! And I'll paint anyone green who disagrees with me."

Some of the things we say about ourselves we have come to believe are actually facts. For years I would say, "I'm not crafty. I can't do crafty things." I thought this was a fact. I was a librarian at a small public library. It would help me if I could learn to do crafts. Eventually, I realized what I believed to be a truth was only words I'd been telling myself. So I tried doing a few things with the kids at my library. After a while, I relaxed and had fun hanging out with the kids and doing crafts.

Remember, you don't have to be "great" at something, you don't have to be the best, and most of the time you don't have to be anything but yourself. Just do it, have fun, and allow for the beauty of imperfection. Most weavers purposely weave a flaw into their tapestries so that the gods/goddesses won't be jealous of them.

Look at your list and see if there is a positive statement you repeat to yourself that you would like to use every time you want to say something nasty to yourself.

For instance: "I am a very creative person. I can dance, dance, dance. I love the color red. Can I create or can I create?"

Decide on a statement that feels good when you read it and practice saying it to yourself. Or use: "I am as I am and you are as you are."

What you say to yourself is more important than what anyone else says.

MAKE A LIST OF NASTIES ABOUT YOURSELF:

_____
_____
_____
_____
_____
_____

REWRITE THOSE NASTIES AS POSITIVES (THEN CROSS OUT THE NASTIES ABOVE):

_____
_____
_____
_____
_____
_____

NOW WRITE A COMPLETELY DIFFERENT POSITIVE LIST:

_____
_____
_____
_____
_____
_____
_____

WRITE A POSITIVE STATEMENT ABOUT YOURSELF:

_____
_____
_____
_____
_____
_____
_____
_____
_____
_____

JOURNAL PAGE:

_____
_____
_____
_____
_____
_____
_____
_____
_____
_____
_____
_____

Money

*Writing is like sex. First you do it for
love, then you do it for your friends,
and then you do it for money.*
first attributed to Ferenc Molnár

*To live sacred lives requires that we live
at the edge of what we do not know.*
Anne Hillman

LET'S GET THIS out of the way. The modern axiom "do what you love and the money will follow" just ain't true. The money may follow, but it may not. Those of us who try to make our living as artists and writers often struggle financially. What Bette Davis said about old age applies to those of us trying to make a buck with our art: "The creative life ain't for sissies."

"The creative life ain't for sissies."

You might as well do work you love, of course, but that doesn't mean you'll make a living doing it.

When I was in college, I asked my writing teacher, Naomi Long Madgett (who is now poet laureate of Detroit) if she thought I had the right stuff to make it as a writer. She said, "Make sure you have a job to bring in some money."

At the time, I thought she was commenting on the quality of my work, so I was determined to ignore her sage advice. Twenty years later as I sat wondering how I was going to pay my electric bill, I realized she had given me very good practical advice. I looked at my husband and asked, "Did it ever occur to you that we would fail? That we wouldn't succeed at making a living at writing?"

"No," he answered.

It had never occurred to me, either.

Of course we hadn't failed. We had done satisfying work and lived the way we wanted. We lived simply compared with most of our contemporaries, which was what we wanted. Yet economically, we always struggled.

In this country, success is spelled m-o-n-e-y. I'm not saying you won't make money. I'm saying it's best if *you* define what success means for you.

Be creative for its own sake—for your own sake. Be creative because the Creative Flow is a natural integral part of your being. And maybe the money will follow.

> You have to define what success means for you.

CREATIVITY TIP

En-Courage yourself. Fill yourself up with courage. To do this, do not denigrate yourself or your art. I once heard Clarissa Pinkola Estés say that denigrating our creativity is the equivalent of soul murder. I agree. Think of it like this: Being nasty to your creations is akin to planting seeds and then stomping on the sprouts once they start coming up. That's not the way to grow plants or creativity. Instead, you sow the seeds, you water the seeds, and when the seeds break open into sprouts, you do what needs to be done to encourage them to keep on growing: Talk to them, add compost, loosen the dirt. Don't fret too much, and let nature take its course. (Yes, sometimes it's as easy as that.) Same with your writing and any other creations. So be kind to yourself and your art.

Journal Page:

Crafty Art

*may earth spinning
be my dance*
Karen Zeiders

IN THE PRIMAL Mind: Vision and Reality in Indian America, Jamake Highwater writes, "For primal peoples . . . the relationship between experience and expression has remained so direct and spontaneous that they usually do not possess a word for art. They do, however, possess a concept of living, which in Western interpretation, might seem like art."

When I read those words twenty some years ago, I was so excited. This was *exactly* how I felt: Life is art and art is life. All those gatekeepers who sat around deciding what was "real" art (i.e. fine art) and what was bad art (craft, or worse yet, folk art) had it all wrong. Art is about life and what we make of it: what we create. It is the act of creation, it is how we feel, it is our connection to the Great Flow that counts when we are making art—making our lives. There is no art with a capital "A" unless all art is Art with a capital "A." There is only Life; there is only Art.

Sometimes you carefully pick up pieces of bark, fallen leaves, bits of shell, a rock or two, bring them home and arrange them in a way that says some-

> We should never forget that many of the artists who are now considered great were revolutionaries about their art.

thing to you, even if you're not certain what. You watch moss grow on rocks, spiders making webs in the curve of the bark, maybe a bird perching on the twig you have sticking out of it all. A storm comes and blows it away, or a deer knocks it over on her way to your garden, or it rots into the ground. You don't mind because you understand the cycle of nature, of life and destruction. You are glad to see your eco-art transform and finally dissolve into something else—it's as if you and Nature were creating this Art together.

I have often heard it suggested that our ancient ancestors left no monuments because they had little culture and no civilization. I believe the monuments they left us were the pristine mountains, uncut forests, and clean rivers and lakes. They created, but they left their mark by not leaving a mark. Maybe all of their art dissolved, maybe all of it transmuted into something more.

I see art and creativity as part of life, not separate from it. I appreciate museums—they allow visual art to be seen by so many people. But museums can also make me uncomfortable because they separate art from people and common life.

We should never forget that many of the artists who are now considered great were revolutionaries about their art. They were often disparaged during their lifetimes. They lived in a world where art was not considered a part of the common existence. Art was for those of the upper class who believed only they could appreciate and understand it.

The American Heritage Dictionary definition of art is "human effort to imitate, supplement, alter, or counteract the work of nature."

That definition makes me shudder. It sounds like they're describing technology, not art. I don't try to imitate, alter, or counteract Nature. I am stepping into my own true Nature and going with the Creative Flow. To alter and counteract Nature to me would be

> **There is only Life; there is only Art.**

> I am stepping into my own true Nature and going with the Creative Flow.

antithetical to true creative process. When I create art, when I am creative, I *am* Nature.

You will hear creative people talk about their "craft" when referring to their work. The definition of craft is "skill or ability in something." It comes from the Middle English "craft" which meant "strength, skill."

Yes. Creativity—craft—is a strength. Christopher Manes writes in his book *Green Rage:*

> Technology confronts the world, forces it to do things it wouldn't do naturally. Craft belongs to a humbler, more ancient relationship with nature—going with the flow. The earth gives up clay and fire, and we make ceramic pots from this bounty. The earth and its non-human communities aren't diminished or banished by the process of craft. Craft fits human needs into the existing landscape.

The word create means "to cause to exist, bring into being." Its root is ker which means "to grow." It has the same root as cereal, and Ceres, the Roman Goddess of agriculture. Patricia Monaghan writes in *The New Book of Goddesses and Heroines*, "Ceres was the force of vegetable growth personified." To step into your Creative Flow is to plant yourself on this Earth, to bring your true self into being—to allow yourself to grow. So let's do it.

CREATIVITY TIP

Plant something. Put it in good soil. Water it when needed. Leave it alone. Watch it grow.

WHAT DID YOU PLANT? HOW DID IT GO? HOW IS IT GROWING?

Journal Page:

Answering the Call Part I

There was a time when you were not a slave, remember that. You walked alone, full of laughter, you bathed bare-bellied. You say you have lost all recollection of it, remember. . . . You say there are no words to describe this time, you say it does not exist. But remember. Make an effort to remember. Or, failing that, invent.
Monique Wittig

BEING CREATIVE OR original is not generally honored or rewarded in our culture, unless of course, you are making lots of money.

We are taught from birth to conform to societal mores and norms. Of course we need some rules and laws to get along in the world with one another. But too often, it seems, peer pressure, advertising, and rules are all about getting us to conform to a norm. Marcos, spokesperson for the Zapatistas, an indigenous insurgency movement based in Mexico, writes in *Our Word Is Our Weapon:*

> Power does indeed want us to be how it wants us to be, to dress in the style it dictates, to talk the way it says we should talk, to eat what it sells, to consider beauti-

> It is more important to live the Truth.

ful and lovely what it considers beautiful and lovely. Power even wants us to love and hate the way it establishes that love and hate should be. Power also wants us to do all this on our knees and in silence, without going around jumping, without shouts, without indigenous uprisings. Power wants us to be well mannered. . . . But the "other" and "different" are not looking for everyone to be like them. . . . Everyone should do their own thing. . . . And in order for this to be possible, it is not enough just to be; you must be while respecting the other. . . . I am as I am and you are as you are. Let's build a world where I can be, and not have to cease being me, where you can be, and not have to cease being you, and where neither I nor you will force another to be like either me or you.

To be creative is to step away from what is expected. It is the beginning of building a world where, as Marcos says, "I am as I am and you are as you are," without either of us ceasing to be ourselves.

To be creative is to question everything you know or think you know. To be creative is to step out of the consumer culture, to stop caring which celebrity is marrying/divorcing which celebrity. To be creative is to stop believing everything you see on TV, on the internet, or in the newspaper. To be creative is to find other sources of Truth.

Be prepared. Family and friends will not necessarily support the new creative you.

"Why can't you be like everyone else?"

Or "Why aren't you like other mothers (fathers, sisters, daughters, etc.)?"

The answer is: *Because*.

Because it is more important to live the Truth.

Because you have planted yourself, because you feel your connection to the Earth.

Because you aren't like other mothers (fathers, sisters, daughters, etc.)

Because it is more fun to be full of yourself.

> To be Creative is to question everything.

CREATIVITY TIP

Create a mile in someone else's shoes. If you normally write from the viewpoint of a woman, write a few paragraphs from the viewpoint of a man, a child, a tree, or a house. Or pick some viewpoint of someone or something you haven't done before. If you're a visual artist, create as someone else. Be Mary Cassatt, Pablo Picasso, or Paul Gauguin. And/or give yourself a pseudonym. Then cook a meal, write a page, draw a picture from the viewpoint of your pseudonymous personality. This can be very liberating.

If writing is your primary creative mode, draw a fairy tale. No stress. No one else has to see it. Draw stick figures if you like. Color them. Make it as fun and colorful as you can.

If visual art is your primary creative mode, rewrite a fairy tale. No stress. No one else has to read it. Have fun with it. Use descriptions. Describe what people are wearing. Describe what they're eating. (If they're wearing a dress, describe the fabric, color, how it feels on the skin. If they're eating cake, describe the texture, color, taste, smell.)

OK. Now go do it.

Draw a fairy tale.

CREATIVITY TIP

Fuggedaboutit.

Don't solicit or expect praise from family. You probably won't get the praise, so why ask or expect it? And even if you do get praise, what does it actually mean? Praise or criticism is one person's opinion. The opinion that matters is your own.

WRITE FROM DIFFERENT VIEWPOINTS:

Journal Page:

DRAW FROM DIFFERENT VIEWPOINTS:

Answering the Call Part II

*It's your road, and yours alone.
Others may walk it with you,
but no one can walk it for you.*
Rumi

YOUR FAMILY AND friends might not be the only ones disconcerted by the new creative you. You should be prepared for these changes in yourself, too, changes that might be uncomfortable.

The Goddess Inanna answered the creative call when she was Queen of Heaven and Earth. First she heard it as a sound. No, it was more of a feeling. A drumbeat. An urging. She followed it—this sound, this feeling, this urge. Followed it until she came to the door to the Underworld. She knew this was not her place. She was, after all, Queen of Heaven and Earth. Still, she knocked. When the Keeper of the Doors opened the door, he looked Inanna up and down and asked her what she wanted. She wasn't sure, so she said, "I'm here to see my sister, Eriskegal. She is Queen of this place. Whatever it is."

"The Underworld," the Keeper said.

"Yes, the Underworld. I'm here to see Eriskegal."

> You should be prepared for these changes in yourself, too, changes that might be uncomfortable.

"There are seven gates," the Keeper of the Doors said. "I require payment before I will let you go through each door."

"Sure, sure," Inanna said. She was, after all, Queen of Heaven and Earth.

At the first door, the Keeper asked for all her Earthly goods. Inanna agreed. At the second door, he asked for all her Heavenly goods. Again she agreed. The urge was so strong now she couldn't resist. Plus, she had been traveling through these doors for days, maybe even years. She was exhausted. Then he asked for all that she believed was true. She agreed. At the fourth door, he asked for her beauty. At the fifth, he wanted her voice. At the sixth, he wanted her clothes. At the seventh, he wanted her shoes.

By the time she handed over her shoes, Inanna could barely stand. She stumbled into the dark dank chamber of the Goddess of the Underworld. By all that Inanna had known before, Eriskegal was ugly. By all that Inanna had known before, She was terrifying. Eriskegal had never been part of the above.

"Why do you come here?" Eriskegal roared.

"I came to see you," Inanna said, falling to her knees.

"I don't believe you!" Eriskegal screamed.

Eriskegal killed Inanna. Just like that. A snap of her fingers. She hung Inanna on a hook for three days. After three days, Inanna's maidservant Ninshubur went looking for help for her mistress. She asked the gods, including Inanna's father, but they all said no. Inanna should never have gone to the Underworld in the first place. How dare she? Finally, Ninshubur got Enki, god of water, wisdom, and Creativity, to help her. He took dirt from under his fingernails and created two little androgynous creatures from the dirt. They then traveled unnoticed to the Underworld where they found Eriskegal moaning.

"Oh my insides!" she cried.

> "I require payment before I will let you go through each door."

"Oh you who are our queen, your insides!" the creatures moaned with her.

"Oh my outsides!" she moaned.

"Oh you who are our queen, your outsides!"

This stopped the Goddess.

"What is it you want?" The Goddess asked the empathetic creatures. When they told her they wanted Inanna, She agreed they may have the corpse. Once they had the corpse, the little creatures sprinkled her with food and water. She slowly revived and left the Underworld with them.

But she was forever changed. She was no longer the beautiful Queen of Heaven and Earth. She was her true-blooded natural self: dark and light. Destroyer and Creatrix. Inanna heard the call, answered it, and found her true powerful Nature. She became "the other." It wasn't always pretty for her.

And it might not always be pretty for you.

> Inanna heard the call, answered it, and found her true powerful Nature.

CREATIVITY TIP

So you've heard the call and you're ready to answer it. Write in your journal what this process feels like. Why you started it, what ideas you're getting, what discomfort you're feeling, what fun you're having. If you don't want to write it, draw it.

Journal Page:

Speaking of Insanity: Addictions

We never know how high we are
Till we are asked to rise
And then if we are true to plan
Our statures touch the skies
Emily Dickinson

> We are being held captive by a culture and a way of being in the world that is unnatural.

LET ME SAY this up front: I don't believe drugs (including alcohol and tobacco) enhance Creativity. Limited use of drugs in ceremony may be beneficial to people in other less addictive cultures, but in Western society, we are constantly struggling with our addictions to alcohol, cocaine, cigarettes, food, television, consumption.

For a long time, I did not understand addictive behavior, including my own. I wondered if these addictions were caused by illness, genetics, chemical imbalance, psychological trauma, or a combination of factors. My own addictive behavior left me feeling helpless and controlled by unhealthy and seemingly unstoppable urges. I felt weak—and alone.

Then I looked around and realized nearly everyone I knew had some kind of addiction, compulsion, or self-destructive behavior. Addictive, destructive behavior had become the norm.

While researching captive animal behavior, I believe I stumbled upon the reason for these kinds of behaviors. Captive animals often develop "zoochosis" and they become "zoochotic" (the animal version of psychotic). These zoochotic animals all exhibit repetitious and/or self-destructive behavior. Bears and elephants develop a kind of obsessive compulsive disorder where they walk in circles, putting their feet in the same spot as they go around and around a circle. Gorillas become bulimic; they eat, throw up, and eat the vomit. Birds pull out their feathers. Chimpanzees, elephants, and bears will rock and sway incessantly.

To become insane seems a natural response to being caged, to being prevented from living a natural free life. Barry Lopez said that a bear in a zoo is a mammal but no longer a bear. Being captive prevents the bear from being a bear.

I believe this has happened to human beings. We are being held captive by a culture and a way of being in the world that is unnatural: We've become zoochotic. When nearly everything we hear, see, and read discourages us from being ourselves—when everything we hear, see, and read tells us we're in big trouble and we feel helpless to do anything about it—we go crazy. For the sake of the planet, our families, and ourselves, we must try to step out of the cage of consumerism, the captivity of "sameness," to become our true wild selves again. To step into the Creative Flow and grow into who we are, we need to step out of our cages.

CREATIVITY TIP

Be still; be quiet; be thoughtless. We all need time to just be. As Mother Star Stupendous Mermaid says in *Church of the Old Mermaids*, "All the wisdom of

> Barry Lopez said that a bear in a zoo is a mammal but no longer a bear.

> We need to listen to the rain or the birds or the refrigerator humming.

the ages can be distilled into one suggestion: Be." And it's true. We all need respite. We all need to stop that hamster-on-the-wheel kind of thinking. We need to listen to the rain or the birds or the refrigerator humming. It doesn't have to be for extended periods of time. Long enough to catch yourself breathing deeply and sinking down into your body. Stillness gives your well of creativity time to fill up again. Go outside in your bare feet and stand on the ground. Squat down and put your hands on the ground. Let all your tension and un-ease drain away.

Journal Page:

Time

You must give birth to your images.
They are the future waiting to be born.
Rainer Maria Rilke

YOU'VE DECIDED TO answer the Creative Call, but you don't have the time. You've got a busy, busy, busy life.

Well, stop it.

You have choices to make. Make them. Are you a consumer of stuff, time, experiences, or are you a citizen of this planet who stops to listen, to be, to learn, to grow?

You've got children, you say. What can you do? They need to do this, that, and the other. Are you teaching them to be consumers of stuff, time, experiences, or to be citizens of this planet?

It's as simple as that.

CREATIVITY TIP

If you feel as though you haven't any extra time, sit down and look at your schedule. And stop saying you don't have any time. That'll put a knot in your stomach. Start saying, "I have plenty of time," or "I have enough time." Ahhh. Doesn't that feel better? Sometimes the motto "fake it until you make it" actually works.

Figure out what you can eliminate so that you put aside time to be creative. If you have children, look at their schedules. You were not put on this Earth to be a martyr to your children. If they're running from this to that to the other activity, they're probably tired, too, and could use some down time, some family time. Figure out how you can all be less busy. You might get resistance and guilt-tripping because the children are used to going, going, going. Gone. Resist their resistance.

Look at your own attitudes toward time-consuming activities like household chores. I have a friend who constantly complains about her spouse never doing anything around the house. When her husband does contribute, she complains that he's done it wrong, and then she steps in and redoes everything. Just because she folded the towels long ways and her husband folded the towels short ways didn't make her right and him wrong. She was wasting everyone's time.

However you need to do it, set aside regular uninterrupted time for your creativity. Make certain your family respects this time and doesn't interrupt you or ask you to change it—and you do the same: Respect yourself and your time.

Respect yourself and your time.

LIST YOUR DAILY OR WEEKLY SCHEDULE:

NOW CROSS OUT EVERYTHING ON YOUR SCHEDULE YOU CAN ELIMINATE

Journal Page:

When and Where

Glorious it is when wandering time is come.
Eskimo song

ANYTIME. ANYWHERE.

That's always been my creative motto. When I was going to college in Michigan in the nineteen seventies, I would drive to Detroit, to the RenCen, and find a cozy spot where I was surrounded by people: talking, walking, eating, laughing people. Then I'd get out my yellow legal pad and a pen and start writing.

I wanted to be able to write anytime, any place.

It's a skill I encourage everyone to foster. Don't wait to be creative until the chores are done, the house is clean, and world peace is achieved.

Do it now.

Accept no excuses from yourself.

Unless they are real excuses.

You know the difference.

I have a friend who swears she will quit smoking once her life settles down. I ask her, "When will that be?" I've known her for over a decade, and she's still smoking.

Years ago, I was in a writing group with a man who said he would start writing his novel once he got a computer. That was all he needed, he said. I told him I wrote on a yellow legal pad, if one was nearby; otherwise, I wrote on whatever I could find, even the bottom of a tissue box. A pen, typewriter, or computer was a tool, nothing more. But it didn't matter what anyone said: He believed he would become a writer, magically, once he had a computer. In the meantime, he could wait.

We can always find reasons to keep smoking or drinking. We can always find reasons not to make time for ourselves. We can always find reasons to keep ourselves from our Creative Flow.

I say make the time anytime, like now.

Make the place anywhere, like here.

> Make the time anytime, like now. Make the place any place, like here.

CREATIVITY TIP

Do something creative in an unexpected time or place. Doodle on your paper napkin in a restaurant. If you're with your family, make it a family thing. Doodle a comic strip. You start. Draw a stick figure, have it say something, then pass the drawing on to the next family member. Be encouraging. If your teenage children are embarrassed, remember it is the obligation of every parent of a teen to embarrass said teen.

Or rearrange your furniture at home. Bring in flowers to work. Wear different clothes, unusual clothes. Cook a meal you've always wanted to cook. Turn on your favorite record and dance around the living room.

Surprise yourself.

Journal Page:

Creative Space

*One cannot think well, love well, sleep well,
if one has not dined well.*
Virginia Woolf

THE GOAL IS to make your Creative Flow a joyful and integral part of your life, but this goal doesn't preclude you from having a room of your own.

In Virginia Woolf's amazing essay "A Room of One's Own," she writes about the creative life and how one needs a place and a time to be creative. She understood that each of us (she spoke of women in particular) needs to have food, shelter, and space to create. With this in mind, you can set aside a creative room for yourself. If you can't have an entire room, make a space for yourself somewhere—even if the space is only in your mind. Ideally, have the space be in a room where you can shut the door behind you. Even if you only have enough room on top of your dresser, do that.

Whether you have a tiny space or an entire room, bring to it objects that make you feel good when you look at them. Pick items from around your house that are meaningful to you. If you have the space, bring in books, boxes of crayons, colored pencils, collage material, or paints.

Don't fill up every inch of space, even if you only

> **Make your Creative Flow a joyful and integral part of your life.**

have a dresser top. Pick one or two things you like to look at and touch: a stone you picked up at the beach, a snake skin someone gave you, a favorite piece of jewelry. The good feelings you have for these objects will rub off on your creativity. They become creative talismans.

Make sure your family or roommates understand this is your space, and they are not allowed to touch any of it. If you have a room where you can actually go, make certain they understand they are not allowed to disturb you when the door is closed except in an emergency. You need to be firm about this—with your kids, mate, and animals.

Your space is your space.

If you really don't have the room for a creative space or for some reason you don't want others to see your space, get a box. Ideally you want to see your creative space and your talismans, but if that can't happen, put your journal, this book, a pen, and a few inspiring objects into the box, then slide it under the bed or put it in the closet where you can easily retrieve it.

The caveat to all of this is that you don't need to have an actual space or place. It is your heart, soul, and imagination that needs the space to wander and find stories and images and beauty. Sometimes creating a space in this world helps us wander in the other worlds, in the imaginal spaces. But don't imprison yourself or your imagination by telling yourself you will be creative only when you have a place and a space. No! Create anytime and in any place.

> It is your heart, soul, and imagination that needs the space to wander and find stories and images and beauty.

CREATIVITY TIP

Kill your TV. Or At Least Temporarily Shut It Off. Turn off the TV, stop watching movies, stop reading fiction. Yep, you heard me right. Deny yourself stories for a while, and you may find new stories turning up in your own imaginal realms. Doesn't have to be forever or even all at once. Try it and see what happens.

Journal Page:

Centering

You can't wait for inspiration.
You have to go after it with a club.
Jack London

YOU'VE GOT THE space. Now close the door and sit a spell. If noise from the rest of the house is going to bother you, put on some soothing instrumental music. No television. No words.

You don't need to formally meditate, but meditation does help the creative process. You can find many books on meditation, so I won't go into the how to do it here. My advice on meditation is the same as my advice for being creative: Just do it. And don't make it complicated.

Before I write, I center myself. Sometimes I meditate for a few minutes. More often, I just imagine a stream of light going down from my spine, into the ground to the center of the Earth. Sometimes I stand in the middle of my room or go outside and turn to the four directions and change the Navajo Beauty prayer to, "I walk in Creativity to the north, I walk in Creativity to the east . . ." Etc.

Whatever you do, don't make it an excuse not to write or paint. In other words, don't say, "I don't have time to center, so I can't write." "I don't know how to meditate, so I can't paint." Centering ourselves, or meditating, is a way to help us more easily access the imaginal realms and our creativity. But it's not something you absolutely have to do. For me, centering and grounding myself makes me more mindful of what I'm about to do. It makes it easier for me to step out of the way and let the stories flow. And that's important: Don't get in your own way.

Keeping our minds clear can be the most challenging part of meditation. It certainly is the most difficult thing for me. I often recite a mantra. A mantra literally means "protection of the mind." A mantra is a recitation of words of power. Although the Buddhists and others use mantras for religious purposes, many people use mantras only to meditate, focus, or center—as a way to clear the mind—without any religious connotations. That's how I use mantras.

OM is considered the Mother of Mantras. The story goes that the goddess Kali Ma uttered OM when she gave birth to the Universe.

I like chanting OM AH HUM. According to Buddhist teacher Tarthang Tulku in his book *Kum Nye Relaxation Part 1,* "OM signifies the energy of existence; AH symbolizes interaction; HUM creativity. OM signifies physical form. AH represents the energy that informs and keeps alive the physical form. HUM symbolizes thoughts, awareness, and activities. OM AH HUM symbolizes the enlightened body, mind, and spirit."

If you don't like OM or OM AH HUM, pick another mantra, preferably not a word that carries a lot of weight for you. The idea is to clear your mind, not get it all stirred up. Let's say you decide to use the word "peace," for instance. If every time you say this word, you think about all the places where war is present, it's not a good word to use. If you use the word love, and every time you whisper it you think about lost love, it's not a good word to use. For me, words are so important and often so fraught with meaning. That's why OM works best for me.

> Don't get in your own way.

Many people use malas to focus their attention while reciting mantras and meditating. In Sanskrit, mala means "garland or roses." Although similar in design to the rosaries Catholics use, Buddhism predates Christianity, and Hinduism predates both. Hindus most likely originated the kind of mala used by Buddhists today with 108 beads. (108 is a significant number in Buddhism for a variety of reasons. A Buddhist teacher told me that using the mala is a way of counting 100 prayers at a time—with eight leftover for any you may have missed or flubbed as you were going around.)

We are overstimulated in this culture. We need to take time away from that over stimulation so we can fill up our creativity wells. Centering, meditation, and chanting helps with that. These kinds of practices help me in the morning, before I jump into the day, or at night before I fall out of the day.

Let the stories flow.

Sometimes it works the other way around. Sitting down and creating can center you. For instance, one night I was having trouble sleeping. I thought if I could settle down, get centered, then I'd be able to sleep. I tried meditating, but it wasn't working. Then I started thinking of my meditation as a poem. I listened to far away noises and then I worked my way back to my body. I wrote down what I heard and called it "Finding Center."

> Train whistle
> Bird song
> Clock ticking
> Ears ringing
> Heart beating

After I wrote it down, I realized I had found my center in spite of myself. What could be more center than my own heart beat? When we create, that's essentially what we're doing whether we know it or not: We're finding center. We go from the universal, to the more local, to our heart: our center. Rooted there, we can reach out again to the local and then to the universal—without thinking about it—and create.

Here's a visualization you can try every now and again before you begin to create:

Sit comfortably with your spine straight and your hands resting on your thighs. Close your eyes. Take deep breaths into your abdomen. Feel yourself relaxing with each breath. Relax your body from the bottom of your feet to the top of your head, from the top of your head to the bottom of your feet. Spend a few minutes doing this.

When you're ready, imagine roots sprouting from the end of your spine and growing into the Earth. Your roots sink deep into the Earth, snaking and twining easily with roots from trees and bushes. Then imagine creative energy flowing from the ground into your roots. This energy goes up your spine as though it's a tree trunk, carrying the energy up through your body until branches sprout from your head and hands.

Raise your hands up to the sky as leaves uncurl from your fingers. Feel the deep grounded connection between the Earth, yourself, and the Cosmos above.

Now imagine the energy flowing back down your arms and your spine and finally your legs until it all flows back into the Earth, leaving you grounded and energized. As you let your arms drop and you rest your hands on your thighs again, know this connection is always with you, providing energy and creativity.

> Imagine roots sprouting from the end of your spine and growing into the Earth.

CREATIVITY TIP

Make your own mala.

What you'll need are some beads or round stones with holes in them and a durable string that'll fit

> You can probably find what you need around the house.

through the holes. It's nice if you can use natural materials, but I'm not trying to get you to go out and buy lots of things. You can probably find what you need around the house. Use 108 beads or pick a number that is significant to you. Whatever you do, make certain you choose stones or beads that feel good to the touch.

When I made mine, I dug up some bean-sized colorful plastic beads from my sewing kit. I sorted them into five colors. I picked an equal number of white, blue, yellow, green, and red beads, and then I added three black beads (to equal 108).

For string, I found a thin piece of leather in the same sewing basket. It only took me about fifteen minutes to string the beads onto the leather strip and then tie the ends together. Voilà! I had my mala.

By the way, when you're knotting the strings, make sure you leave some room between the beads so that they move easily between your thumb and finger as you chant.

Journal Page:

Perspective

*We can complain because rose bushes have thorns,
or rejoice because thorn bushes have roses.*
Abraham Lincoln

*Some people see the glass half full. Others
see it half empty. I see a glass that's
twice as big as it needs to be.*
George Carlin

GET A NEW perspective. Get many new perspectives.

Begin with your own life. See if you can start viewing your life as your art.

Think about something you have a strong opinion about, maybe something to do with politics, for instance. Now argue the other side to yourself. And be convincing. Do this with all kinds of things. If you like classical music and hate country music, make the argument that country music is great.

Go to the room where you spend the most time. Sit where you usually sit and look around the room, letting your gaze rest on the various walls, corners, and objects in the room. Listen. What do you hear? Do you smell anything? Move your fingers and feet. What do you feel beneath them? How do you feel sitting there?

Now get up and stand or sit somewhere in the

> See if you can start viewing your life as your art.

room where you rarely go. Look around the room. Notice any differences. Do you hear anything different here? Smell? What do you feel beneath your fingertips and feet? How do you feel?

Do this in other parts of the house. Go out in your yard and find places to be where you usually don't go. Use all your senses and discover new things about old places.

A few years ago, I entered some of my art pieces in a juried art show at the local library. My pieces didn't get in. At first I was depressed. I started doubting my abilities. But that line of thinking was getting me nowhere.

So I decided to put on my own art show in my house at the same time as the library's art show in October. Halloween is my favorite holiday, so I called it the Hallows Art Show. I asked people to create art centered around the theme of Halloween: honoring the dead, celebrating the harvest and the turning of the Wheel of the Year, and creating whatever other art October inspired.

I wanted to give my friends an excuse to go with the flow and create something for an art show without a gatekeeper—or at least with a gatekeeper who said, "Welcome, I honor you, I honor your Art." I invited friends I believed would be open to the idea. Not all of these people considered themselves artists. All the better.

What a great success it was. The show had 38 pieces in it from seventeen different people. We wrote, designed, and printed a catalog of the show, complete with biographies of the artists. I assembled the pieces in our house to create a visual trip to the Underworld and out again. The living room was the waiting room to the Underworld.

The next room, ordinarily my workroom, was the Underworld, where most of the artwork was on display. After leaving the Underworld, the back room became a Dumb Supper Room where a long table

> Use all your senses and discover new things about old places.

was set with various "place setting" art pieces. After the Dumb Supper Room, the kitchen was the next stop. Even after a trip to the Underworld, one must get nourishment. *Especially* after a trip to the Underworld.

Our art show had found objects, raku, baskets, tempera paintings, masks, a quilt made by my father, a pillow made by my mother, aroma therapy oils, Day of the Dead necklaces and earrings, scarves, a mannequin of death, and a smaller mannequin, all in white, called *Her Spirit Returns*.

It was an amazing experience and a huge hit in the community. After the grand opening (and a great party), we left the show up for the entire month. People came all month to my house and wandered around the art show. Our artists sold lots of their pieces, too.

And maybe some people in the community got a new perspective on what Art is. I certainly did. Several people thanked me for encouraging them to think creatively about their lives and to effectively give them permission to be creative.

CREATIVITY TIP

Write a description.

Description is important in nearly all writing. Too much of it can slow down a narrative, especially in fiction. Too little of it can unground your reader, and then they lose interest in your narrative.

Many writers struggle with description. (Even if you're not a writer, this exercise can help open up your creative doors.) If you're one of the writers who gets stymied by description, try this trick I learned from Mario: When you come to a place in the narrative that needs description but you're not ready to write it, type in "tk" and keep on writing. (It's an editing mark that means "to come.") You can go back later, keyword search your manuscript for "tk", and fill it in then.

To my way of thinking, the best kinds of descriptions are the ones with the least amount of words. Most of the time, you're actually trying to evoke a memory in the reader of something she/he already knows. In other words, you're not trying to describe every single *thing*. When you write "chair," you understand that most readers will know what a chair is. Say you're trying to describe a meal. Unless you're writing a food article or a scene where you're focusing on the food, you want your description to be short and sweet, so to speak. At this particular meal, you had curry chicken, but you didn't care for it. How could you describe this in one sentence?

"The curry chicken had a chalky taste that comes from too much cinnamon."

Most people know what cinnamon tastes like and understand it ain't good when there's too much of it. So you don't actually have to describe the taste of cinnamon. To make it more interesting, you can play with that description to sum up the entire meal. Of course, the tone and wording changes depending upon the narrator.

"The conversation wasn't much better than the chalky-tasting curry chicken they served us."

"The conversation made me gag almost as much as the cinnamony curry chicken. Bleck."

"The dull conversation could have used some of the spice that made the chicken taste like chalk."

You get the idea.

Description is all about context. You don't want the reader distracted by your descriptions. You want them immersed in the story or essay. I prefer my fiction and nonfiction without a lot of adjectives. Here's a part of a description I wrote after witnessing a lightning storm. Most people have seen lightning and know what an x-ray is, so I played with that:

"Lightning zigzagged through the sky, as though some strange X-ray machine was switching on and off to show us the truth of the world—or at least the

Description is all about context.

truth of the sky: There be dragons here. And power. And brilliance."

With poetry, you can continue to play with metaphor and analogy, which I like to do. This is from my poem, "Rose Red and Snow White" (about the fairy tale of the same name).

> When Le Bête knocks on their door
> Mid-winter, matted ice and snow giving him
> A Rasti look, the twin goddesses invite
> The Wild in,
> Serve him tea and comb his fur.
> No sign of gold at first blush.

Even if someone has no idea what Rastafarian dreadlocks look like, most people will get the idea from the "matted ice and snow."

So, for your exercise, write a description of a place, person, object, or animal. First write a paragraph. Then cut the paragraph down, getting rid of as many adjectives as you can while maintaining the essence of your perception. Do this several times: describing the same person, place, or thing. Then do it for something else. Have fun with it.

Many writers struggle with description.

DESCRIPTIONS:

Journal Page:

Creative Cycles

*Art is the only way to run away
without leaving home.*
Twyla Tharp

EVERYTHING HAS A rhythm. Each season has its own rhythm. The waxing and waning of the moon is cyclical. You have your own daily, monthly, and yearly rhythms, too. Your creativity can be enhanced when you know and understand your own rhythms.

Because of the way most modern people live, few of us are in sync with our own rhythms. We sleep too little, wake up to noise (alarm clocks), and go to bed tired. We are not encouraged to live our lives according to our natural rhythms. We are taught to be the same and act the same at all times. No ups and downs. Peaks and flows. But we are biological creatures—not robots—and we *are* cyclical creatures.

Think about your own rhythms, patterns, and cycles. You are probably already aware of some. What time of day do you feel the sharpest? The most tired? The most creative?

Mario gets up two hours before work and writes for an hour. This is his solitary creative time. I'm happily still sleeping at 6:00 a.m. while he works. He figured out that he can best go with the flow if he writes in the morning. That's when the writing comes

> Think about your own rhythms, patterns, and cycles.

easiest for him. When he waits until the afternoon, writing is more difficult.

I have more energy in the morning, but not at 6:00 a.m. From 10:00 to 2:00 I can get a lot done. After lunch, I'm sleepy. I get a surge of energy after dinner, but if I work much after 9:00 p.m. I have trouble sleeping. This knowledge of my own rhythms helps me decide that I shouldn't try to write or do other creative things after lunch. And even though I have the energy to keep working late at night, it disturbs my sleep patterns, so I don't work then.

What about you?

We have monthly and seasonal cycles, too. (Yes, whether you are male or female, you've got cycles.) At one time of year, we may feel more gregarious than we do at other times. Some days we feel nice. Some days (or weeks) we don't feel so nice.

It is natural to have a variety of reactions to the ups and downs of our lives. For instance, we may need the extra push of crankiness or irritation so that we can recognize when we are being treated poorly or other people are acting recklessly or disrespectfully. The part of the cycle that pinches us, so to speak, that irritates us, provides us with the energy or words we need to call our county engineer's office, for instance, to try to get them to stop roadside pesticide spraying; it helps us write letters to our elected representatives to urge them to protect our environment; it helps us tell our children they need to treat us better. It helps us stand up for ourselves and our community, to be willing and ready to rock the boat no matter how many people are accusing us of "not being nice."

Mario has trouble sleeping once or twice a month. This restlessness almost always correlates with either the full or the new moon. When I pointed this out to him, he said he couldn't imagine why the phase of the moon would affect his sleep patterns. I

If you are tired, rest. If you are hungry, eat. Listen to your body.

didn't know why either, but if the moon can affect the Earth's tides, why not us?

And yearly? Are there some seasons you look forward to more than others? Some times of the year when you feel more energetic than others?

One of my sisters, who is very social most of the year, hardly sees anyone during the winter months. She isn't depressed; she says she feels like hibernating in the winter. I have a great deal of energy in the early fall; however, I am most creative in the spring and summer. It is then I want to write, take photos, make pictures, and work in my garden. I am not particularly social with people in the spring and summer. I want to be outside but not necessarily with anyone. Late summer and early fall, I get this peculiar burst of energy when I suddenly want to be with other people. This is when I usually plan parties. Then in November, I begin to withdraw. December I get social for the holidays, but not in a frenetic way. We celebrate the changing of the seasons quietly. Then I'm happy not to have much social contact until March.

My cycles—all of them—are related to the natural world. I am a biological being. You are, too. I try to follow my natural rhythms as much as I can.

When we feel like hibernating, for instance, it's probably what we need, body and soul: a time out from our problems and the world's problems. Honor that. Give yourself space to be a biological creature. Mario will often read late, even though he is clearly tired and needing sleep. I say, "If your body wants sleep, sleep." He forces himself to stay awake because he thinks sleeping is a waste of time; his body thinks differently and tries to tell him this with yawns and droopy eyes.

I say if you are tired, rest. If you are hungry, eat. Listen to your body. It is important to become attuned to your rhythms so that you can determine when it is easiest for you to be creative. Mario figured out early mornings were his best times. When he wrote poetry

> Your creativity can be enhanced when you know and understand your own rhythms.

in the morning, it was like being on a river in a boat, sailing easily with the wind. In the afternoon, it was like being on a river in a boat sailing against the wind and against the current. It took a lot more energy, and it wasn't fun. You want to find a time of the day (and the month and the year) that is easiest and best for *your* Creative Flow.

CREATIVITY TIP

Track your daily, month, yearly cycles in your journal. Give yourself permission not to be the same every day. Give the people around you the same permission (especially if you live with teenagers). This may be something you have to say out loud many times, for yourself and your family.

Start paying attention to the natural world. Remember you are part of Nature. Watch the trees in your environment to see when they bud out, how long the leaves are green, when they change colors, when they fall. Even desert and evergreen trees display discernible cyclical changes.

If you can, go out in the country and walk the same path at least once a week. Note what you see. How does the area change? Evolve? Grow? Write or draw your observations in your journal afterward, but while you are on the trail, it is important to be there. Don't be in your head deciding what you'll write about. In fact, if you find yourself doing that, talk yourself out of it. If you can't stop the mental chatter, decide not to write about your walk at all and enjoy yourself.

Start paying attention to the natural world.

CREATIVITY TIP

Get Inspired.

Use anything and everything for inspiration. And don't worry about perfection or doing it "right." I know I keep saying this, but it bears repeating. Creativity is not about perfection or doing it right. Of course there are jobs where you need to get it right, and you need to strive for perfection. If you're doing

Being creative is a way of life.

brain surgery, then yes, you want to do it perfectly. Creativity isn't one of those "jobs." In fact, it's not a job. Being creative is a way of life. It's a way of being. Part of this way of being includes finding inspiration everywhere and anywhere.

Cycles:

JOURNAL PAGE:

Dreams

Sleep is the best meditation.
Dalai Lama

IF YOU DON'T already pay attention to your dreams, start. You don't have to do this forever; try it for a while, maybe a month or two. Then keep doing it if you want, stop if you don't.

Keep paper and pen by your bed so you can write down a few sentences about the dream before you get up. I often wake up from dreams in the middle of the night. I'm too sleepy to write the entire dream coherently in my journal then, so I'll jot down key words on the loose paper by my bed—words that I hope will help me recall the dream once I wake up for the day.

When you write out your dreams do it in present tense. "I was walking down the street and suddenly x, y, or z happened." This sense of immediacy can help you remember more detail.

If a particular dream seems important to you, if it bothers you, scares you, or delights you, try working with it. Draw it in your journal, using crayons or colored pencils. Share it with someone who is interested in dreams (but not someone who will tell you what they believe the dream means). Extend the dream—keep writing the dream as if you had kept dreaming it, like adding to a story. See if the dream is saying something to you.

I don't recommend using dream dictionaries, especially if you're new to dream watching. I dreamed once a tooth fell out. I looked it up in a dream book and having a tooth fall out meant I was going to die soon. Scared the crap out of me. Your brain or your mind or your being is coming up with the images in your dreams, so what you think they mean is more important than what anyone else says.

After you've been looking over your dreams for a time, you might try a dream dictionary as long as you are using it only as a guide and not as the ultimate source of truth. I like Patricia Telesco's *The Language of Dreams*. She usually gives a variety of interpretations based on different cultures.

Mario believes dreams are random neuron firings, with just about that much meaning. Mario rarely remembers his dreams, but when he does, they seem so symbolic to me. For instance, once he dreamed he was a baker and was worried about having enough bread. At the time, Mario was worried about the amount of money he was making. Money = dough = bread.

I don't really know what dreams are. I have had vivid dreams all of my life, many in one night. I have gone through long periods where I have had several nightmares a night. I have inspiring dreams, too. If I watch something scary on television, I'll have nightmares. If I eat sugar before bed, I'll have nightmares. When I was studying Buddhism, I had Buddhist dreams. When I was studying Jung, I had Jungian dreams. Sometimes my dreams give me insight into what's going on in my life, other times I haven't a clue as to what they mean.

I don't know why we dream. So why pay attention to them when you're trying to be more creative? Because they are part of who we are. They are mysterious, often unexplainable, creative and mystical

> If a particular dream seems important to you, if it bothers you, scares you, delights you, try working with it.

just as they are. I see them as gifts, whole and complete as they are. If nothing else, use your dreams as a source of inspiration for a story, painting, or musical composition. Think about starting a dream journal.

CREATIVITY TIP

Most people don't get enough sleep. They also don't get enough good sleep. Scientists have recently determined sleeping in complete darkness is better for our health. Our immune systems need the darkness in order to produce melatonin which helps protect us from different types of cancer. Even a little bit of light around your bed (including your television set) can cause your immune system to stop producing melatonin and instead produce other "daytime" hormones.

> Dreams are mysterious, often unexplainable, creative and mystical just as they are.

If you see any light when you turn out the lights at night, figure out a way to cover it up. We have shades in our bedroom, but light from the street seeped in along the sides of the window. I got a black cloth and hung it over the shades. Then we also close the bathroom door and the door to Mario's study so that no light comes in from those sources. We do take down the covering for the three nights of the full moon (the night before, the night of, and the night after), so that we can sleep by the light of the moon those nights—imitating as best we can what it would be like to sleep with natural lighting.

Try to fall to sleep in darkness. If you get up in the middle of the night, try not to turn on any lights if you can. Once those lights come on, the melatonin switches off.

Sleeping better in darkness will help your immune system, you'll awaken better rested, and you'll feel more creative.

CREATIVITY TIP

Work fast. Robert Louis Stevenson wrote *The Strange Case of Dr. Jekyll and Mr. Hyde* in three weeks. Muriel Spark completed *The Prime of Miss Jean Brodie* in one month. Franz Kafka regularly wrote short stories in a single sitting. Charles Dickens composed *A Christmas Carol* in six weeks. There are many more examples of enduring works of literature written in a short time. Writing quickly short-circuits the critical part of your brain and allows you to access the creative core. If you're used to writing slowly, give rapid writing a try. You might be surprised by the result.

Work fast!

Write quickly:

DRAW QUICKLY:

Journal Page:

Getting Physical

There is a vitality, a life force, an energy, a quickening that is translated through you into action, and because there is only one of you in all time, this expression is unique. And if you block it, it will never exist through any other medium and it will be lost.
Martha Graham

THE BEST THING you can do for your creativity is to do something physical, the more of it outdoors the better. If you physically can't do much, don't worry. I wrote my first published novel when I was so sick I could barely sit in the chair to write. So if you are sick, know that you are still creative and can continue to do creative work. But I know from experience that it is easier to be creative when you can move your body.

Moving your body is inspiring. Moving your body shakes loose inhibitions. Moving your body shakes loose fear. Moving your body can shake up all those wonderful ideas and make them more accessible to you.

So move it!

You can hike, ride a bike, or play tennis.

You could also dance. That's one of my favorite activities. Turn on music you like, music that you have to move it, and get up and dance. If you don't feel comfortable dancing around anyone else, do it when the house is empty. Or do it in your creative space with the door closed. But move. First move those hips and then everything else will follow. You need to swing those hips, too. Women *and* men. Feel the music and go with it.

I've watched people dance. So have you. Some people get this lost faraway look in their eyes. They are self-conscious and want to be somewhere else. Other people smile and laugh and don't seem to care who is watching. I want you to be smiling and laughing. Don't dance by rote. Feel the sound waves in the bare soles of your feet. Move your body to the rhythm of music. If you feel uncomfortable or self-conscious, turn up the music. Or close your eyes. It is only you and the music.

And when it's windy, go outside and dance with the wind. It is so much fun being outside dancing with the wind, the trees, the birds, and the bees. In the summer, the swallows hunting for insects will dive down and dance with you.

Use every opportunity you have to dance. Dance while cooking. Dance while walking. Make the entire day a dance.

Or dance in your creative space, just you and the music. Get used to your body feeling the music.

Yes!

CREATIVITY TIP

Go outside. Get into nature. When you're walking in the forest or the desert or along a seashore, it is important to be present to the experience. Don't get lost in that hamster-on-a-wheel kind of thinking. If you can't be outside, do something physical indoors. Do whatever you are physically able to do. Try to work up a sweat.

> **Use every opportunity you have to dance!**

Journal Page:

Nature and The Invisibles

Some say that sudden knowledge of mystical matters is accomplished only in complete quietude, or that Creator, in one of God's many forms, appears only in orderly ways that are beauteous and picturesque, or that the mystical appears only in completely silent ways. All are true. Except for the "only" part.
Clarissa Pinkola Estés

> Everything spoke to me: the wind, trees, animals, my imaginary friends.

WHEN I WAS a girl everything spoke to me: the wind, trees, animals, my imaginary friends. I left meat out for the hawks and stood at the edge of the marsh and called to the *ignis fatuus,* the foolish fire. I sat in trees, talking and singing to them all the time. It didn't trouble me that my four sisters didn't talk to the trees or animals or invisible friends. I felt a part of the natural world I loved so much.

When I became a teenager, I started to worry that something was wrong with me because I heard and felt things other people did not. No one I knew lived in an alternative universe in their head. No one talked to trees or named rocks. One day when I was about sixteen years old, I gave up—my "imaginary" world, and I gave up my friendships with the marsh, trees, hawks, and clouds.

It took me many years before I connected with Nature again. Once I did, my creative life took off.

For me, stories come from the ground up, so I need frequent and direct connection with the wild. I also find Nature when I'm in the city. I change my perspective and expectations a bit. I might not see a bear in Portland, but I can connect with some pretty cool trees, birds, and human beings.

Some years ago when we were in New Mexico, we spent a day with Dr. Clarissa Pinkola Estés (author of *Women Who Run With the Wolves*), along with a couple hundred other people. She sat on the stage and spun stories around us, like a magical weaver creating shawls of inspiration for each of us using only her words. She talked about stepping out of what we know. Move. Don't be afraid of what others think. Be yourself. Do not denigrate your intuitions—to do so was murder on creativity, she said. "Creativity is enhanced when what is invisible is acknowledged," she told us.

I agree. We need to give ourselves permission to listen to our intuition, to the trees, the wind. This isn't supernatural, this is absolutely natural. Don't worry that it's not scientific. Science doesn't know everything. Many things in Nature are invisible but measurable: wind, radiation, electromagnetic fields. How much is invisible but not measurable on any scientific equipment?

For instance, I am certain that the cottonwood at the Turtle Pond knows me and dances with the wind to say hello whenever I come to visit. When I hike in the woods on rainy days, I ask the wind and rain and clouds to please not rain on me until I return to the car, if it'll cause harm to none. Since I started doing this, I have only been rained on once, lightly, for the last five minutes of a walk. (I always thank the rain for holding off so long.)

In the winter of 1996, we experienced awesome weather here in the Pacific Northwest. We had snow, ice storms, a warming trend, torrential rains, and historical flooding all in one month. One night after

> This isn't supernatural, this is absolutely natural.

> See the world as living. This helps the creative process.

watching the volunteer fire department pump out my neighbor's basement in an attempt to save it from the flooding Columbia River, I sloshed through the water to get home, surrounded on all sides by historical flooding. Once I was on my porch, I looked up at the rain clouds and said, "I know I don't know much, but if it won't cause harm to anything, do you think you could please let up? We're all feeling quite stressed, and the flooding is causing all kinds of environmental harm. What do you think?" The next day the rain stopped, and the river began going down.

Last night as I fell to sleep, I said, "I really would like to wake up to the sound of coyotes." And I did. It was full moon, and I awakened to hear the coyotes singing—only for a minute for the first time in years—and then I went back to sleep.

I don't tell you these stories to demonstrate I'm all powerful (because I'm not) but to suggest that communication with the invisible, as well as the visible, is possible. I believe life wants communication, whether it's a tree or a frog or the wind—or myself. And for me, the more time I spend in Nature, the more creative I am.

Creativity Tip

Go outside and communicate with a plant. Hug a tree or sit by plant and see what you discern. Hear anything? Feel anything? Don't judge the experience. Don't try. Just be with yourself and this plant. You may feel silly. But go ahead. Relax. Have a conversation with the plant, either out loud or in your imagination. (Depends upon who's listening, eh?) If you like, afterward, write down the conversation and/or draw the plant.

If you don't like the idea of talking to plants, go outside and imagine mythological creatures are walking over the land where you are standing. See them in your mind's eye if you can. Hear them. Smell them. Imagine them however you can. Then focus on one mythological creature in particular. Have a conversation with her in your imagination. After a few minutes, draw or write about the experience.

Don't judge your conversation or drawings. The purpose of these exercises is to get you to see that the world is alive. This realization helps the creative process. It helps the *living* process.

> Don't judge your conversation or drawings.

COMMUNICATING WITH NATURE:

Journal Page:

Creation Stories

*There is no greater agony than bearing
an untold story inside you.*
Maya Angelou

"Stories connect us to the universe of medicine—of paranormal or sacred power," Paula Gunn Allen writes in her book *Grandmothers of the Light*.

Clarissa Pinkola Estés writes in "The Medicine of the Tales" in *Tales of the Brothers Grimm*, "The most imperishable and wise ideas are gathered together in the silvery nets we call stories."

Victorian folk tale anthologists "regularly subverted and subsumed the stories that starred strong and illustrious female heroes, promoting instead those stories that showed women as weak or witless or, at the very best, waiting prettily and with infinite patience to be rescued," Jane Yolen writes in "The Female Hero and the Women Who Wait," her forward to Kathleen Ragan's *Fearless Girls, Wise Women, and Beloved Sisters*.

"Traditional fairy tales are drawn from many sources, including ancient mythology, pagan religion, political allegory, morality plays, and Orientalia. Most such tales have filtered through centuries of patriarchal culture and show little respect for women," Barbara G. Walker writes in *Feminist Fairy*

> We each have our own creation story.

Tales.

I believe these writers are correct. Fairy tales, myths, and legends all contain gems of truth, often covered by the ash of thousands of years of rewriting to fit certain world views. Whenever one culture takes over another, one of the first things they do is rewrite history. In times past, that meant rewriting myths and fairy tales.

Athena was originally a Minoan or Mycenaean goddess, a household goddess, represented by the serpent who protected the house's stores against rats. When the Greeks became the conquerors of this part of the world, Athena became connected to Pallas, a Greek warrior goddess. Pallas Athena was born from the head of Zeus, the legend was told. This new legend did a number of things.

First, Athena becomes a motherless goddess. The Minoan and Mycenaean civilizations were more egalitarian, women-oriented—in other words, mother-oriented—than the Greeks. When the patriarchal Greeks took over, they didn't want any powerful matrifocal people to deal with. So they killed off Athena's mother, who represented her matrifocal past. Now she's born from Zeus, and her only parent is male.

The Greeks also made Athena a virgin, since the patriarchal societies were obsessed with making certain women didn't have pleasurable sex, often raping their women (and goddesses) in their legends. Yet they wanted to keep Athena because the general populace had great affection for her and looked to her for protection. They could use this affection and trust of the goddess for their own means by rewriting her creation story. This process is often politely called syncretism: the attempt or tendency to combine or reconcile differing beliefs, as in philosophy or religion.

Most of the fairy tales we hear or read today were

> Fairy tales, myths, and legends are all gems of truth.

once pagan and have been sifted through Judeo-Christian filters.

Each of us knows many creation stories. We learn the story of the Universe, the story of our country, our town, our family. All of these stories change and evolve over the years, with events and ideas added and taken away, lies told and lies explained, truths told and untold.

In addition, we each have our own creation story. Most of us know where we were born, to which parents, where we grew up, and how we responded to the world. These are the stories told to us by our families and friends and stories we tell ourselves. These tales have great power, just as other myths and fairy tales have great power. We come to believe them even when they are not wholly true.

Here's an example of what I mean. Part of my family creation story goes like this. I was born in Shreveport, Louisiana, while my parents were in the service there. We moved back to Michigan when I was about two years old. My grandfather and father built our house. When I was about five years old, I was sprawled on a pile of clean clothes in front of our dryer. My father told me to get up. When I wouldn't, he took hold of my hand and I, being the "brat" I was, jerked away from him. My shoulder was dislocated, and my father took me to the hospital where they asked him all kinds of embarrassing questions.

For years, whenever this story was told, the brat part was emphasized. The horrible part of the story wasn't that my shoulder was dislocated, and I was screaming in pain, but that I had embarrassed my father by getting my shoulder dislocated, thereby causing those hospital people to accuse my father of child abuse. When I retold this story to friends, I always said what a brat I was.

Later in life, I looked at my birth certificate and discovered that I had actually been born in Bossier City, not Shreveport. When I asked my father why

> **Whenever one culture takes over another culture, one of the first things they do is to rewrite history.**

they had told me my whole life that I had been born in Shreveport, he said it was because we had lived in Shreveport and the hospital was in Bossier City, on the base. So there was one truth revealed, an innocent mistake. But for thirty years on every form I had ever filled out, I had put in the wrong place of birth.

And what about me getting my shoulder dislocated? Was that a true story? A friend of mine told me children often dislocate their shoulders. Her son had done so while climbing a tree. However, in my case, I did not dislocate my shoulder because I was a brat. Most likely what happened is I was angry and my father was angry and he pulled too hard on my hand while I was pulling away. He didn't mean to hurt me, and he was embarrassed and felt bad about the incident. My parents did what most people do when they aren't the hero in a story: They rewrote it. They told the "brat" story so my father would always be blameless. What harm could there be in that?

The harm in that was I grew up believing I *was* a brat who constantly caused my parents great shame and unhappiness. I believed that story and all others where I "caused" grown-ups to hurt me or behave badly.

Family stories are powerful. But we can change them. We can write our own creation stories.

Think about what your creation story is now. Draw it or write it out. Explore your entire life if you can. You're not trying to psychoanalyze yourself or relive bad times. No! From as neutral a viewpoint as you can manage, figure out what stories you and others have told about you.

Write it out as simply or as complicated as you want. Mine went like this: "I made my entrance into the world on a humid March morning not far from the Red Chute Bayou and Red River, inside a hospital on Barksdale Air Force Base where my father was stationed in Bossier City, Louisiana. Although I came screaming into this world amidst stainless steel

> **Family stories are powerful. But we can change them.**

and concrete, I like to think my first breath sucked swamp gas and Voodoo dust into my baby lungs."

Short or simple, give yourself some space and time to do this writing or drawing.

When you're finished, ask yourself if you're happy with that creation story. What would you change? For instance, perhaps you wish you had been taught different skills: to be self-confidant, to be gentle, to be joyful. Or maybe you wish your parents had acted differently. It's all right, you can think these things. This is your own private musing. Nothing terrible is going to happen to you or your parents or anyone else because you are assessing the strengths and weaknesses of your life.

Now try to think of a fairy tale, legend, or myth that you really enjoy. Choose some story you've always thought was powerful. Find it and read it again. Read it out loud if you can. See if you still like it. (Snow White may have sounded good when you were eight, but now the idea of waiting for Prince Charming to make it all better may seem a bit silly.)

What if you become the hero/hera of that story? How does it feel? Read it out loud now putting you in the role of the main character. Did you still like it? What if you tweaked some of the details to fit more closely to your world view or the world view you'd like to have.

One of my favorite stories is "The Crescent Moon Bear." Clarissa Pinkola Estés has a Japanese version of it in *Women Who Run With the Wolves*. I've read many versions. Sometimes it's a bear, sometimes a tiger.

The skeleton of the story is essentially the same. A man comes home from the war, and he is very angry. His wife tries to care for him, but he won't have anything to do with her. She goes to the healer at the edge of the village and asks for a potion to make her husband well. The healer agrees but says she needs a hair from the chin of the crescent bear (or the eyelash

> A wonderful—and simple—way to give yourself a new creation story is to provide yourself with some fairy god or goddess mothers.

of a tiger or the scale of the fierce serpent) who lives atop the mountain.

The woman agrees to get it. She must face many obstacles, But she loves her husband so much she would do anything for him. Finally she reaches the top of the mountain and the cave where the fierce bear lives. Every night she leaves him a bowl of food and stands far away while he eats it. Each time she puts down a new bowl of food for him, she moves a little closer to the bear.

Finally she is close enough so that the bear sees her. He struts around roaring and showing his teeth, but she stands her ground. She reminds him that she has fed him for many days; now, could she have one of his hairs in payment so the healer can make a potion to cure her husband? The bear agrees.

The woman plucks out the hair and hurries back down the mountain. She gives the hair to the healer who immediately tosses it into the fire where it burns up. The woman is horrified. The healer assures her all is well. She tells her to remember each step she took on her journey to retrieve the hair, remember everything she learned including patience and courage, remember all that and take this knowledge home with her and use her newfound wisdom when dealing with her husband.

I made this story into a kind of creation story of my own called "Dragon Pearl" after a difficult visit home to see my family. I was frustrated that I could be a woman in her forties who still felt undone in the presence of her family. At the time of my visit, my parents were both ill. I would have given almost anything to make them better, but I couldn't do anything, and they weren't particularly thrilled at having me there.

In my rewrite, the shy self-sacrificing hera went to the village healer because her parents were ill. The healer sent her to retrieve the legendary dragon pearl which dragons protected with their lives. She

> This is your own private musing.

climbed the mountain, befriended the dragon, did a favor for the dragon who then gifted her with the dragon pearl.

Because of her travails, she discovered her true self. And when she returned to her parents, they didn't treat her any differently, but she felt better about her interactions with them because she was a different person.

When you put yourself into a new creation story, the purpose is not to make everything easy for you, but to give yourself the skills to cope with whatever comes your way.

I went to a workshop once with Vicki Noble and Demetra George at Breitenbush deep in the Oregon woods. Surrounded by natural hot springs and tall cedars, we studied the ancient Amazons. When I was a kid, I was taught that the powerful women warriors were mythological, but I've since come to believe (along with some scholars, historians, and archeologists) that the Amazons may have been real women. (See archaeologist Jeannine Davis-Kimball's chapter on the Amazons in *Warrior Women*.)

In the workshop we were given a list of names of Amazon women. I picked a name I liked. I remember walking under the grand old cedar trees through a snowy silence to my cabin, and I imagined my life as an Amazon—as if I had actually been born an Amazon. I imagined being encouraged to be strong, courageous, and to stand up for myself. In this new creation story, no one ever told me to sit still or be nice. I grew up to become a great archer, tracker, naturalist, and diplomat who was able to take care of myself and my community. By the time I reached my cabin, I felt very powerful and self-assured. I liked this new creation story.

So write, draw, or color yourself a new creation story. You can take an old fairy tale or legend and put yourself in it as the main character. Or take a tale and tweak it like I did with "Dragon Pearl," with you

> Nothing terrible is going to happen to you or your parents by assessing the strengths and weaknesses of your life.

as the central character. Or write (or draw) yourself a new story that you like better than the one you've grown up with.

I know this sounds big, especially if you've never written anything before. But try and relax with it. It doesn't have to be perfect. No one else is going to read this story except you. It isn't about you writing something beautiful and poetic in someone else's eyes. This is all for you.

You don't even have to use words if you don't want to. Instead use a crayon to draw the story as you tell the story out loud to yourself.

And your new creation story need only be about your beginnings if you like. You don't have to rewrite your entire last sixty years, for instance. Or your last twenty. Rewrite your beginning if that's all you want to do.

A wonderful—and simple—way to give yourself a new creation story is to provide yourself with some fairy god or goddess mothers who give you many gifts at the beginning of your life, gifts that you may have forgotten or didn't know about until just this moment.

You can keep your same parents in this creation story if you want. This could be my creation story: I was born March 25 in Bossier City, Louisiana. I came into this world as sister to Karen and daughter to Lloyd and Mary. My parents were so happy I had been born to them that they had a beautiful and elaborate naming ceremony for me. To this naming ceremony they invited thirteen goddessmothers. These women—old, young, middle-aged, dark, light—came from here and there and everywhere. The first goddessmother brought me a charm bracelet and put on this bracelet a tiny clown's hat. This represented the gift of foolishness and good humor she gave me as she kissed my forehead. "No matter what situation you ever find yourself in," she told me, "you'll be able to laugh and not take yourself too seriously."

When you put yourself into a new creation story, the purpose is not to make everything easy for you, but to give you the skills to cope with whatever came your way.

Don't forget the gift of creativity.

The second goddessmother added a tiny replica of a roaring fire onto the charm bracelet. "May you always be blessed with the energy to make your way in the world, with the ability to discover your passions and go ahead with them." She kissed me on the forehead, too. The third goddessmother slipped a tiny silver Amazon axe on my bracelet. "May you have great strength, my child, and the ability to take care of yourself."

And so it goes. You get the idea. It is a wonderful way to gift yourself (via the mothers) with whatever you need in life. Don't forget the gift of creativity.

Creativity Tip

Read fairy tales from a variety of cultures. If you haven't rewritten your creation story yet, I encourage you to go ahead and do so. Rewrite it as yourself, and then rewrite as if you were an Amazon. There is some evidence that the Amazons were not only part of Greek myth. They may have been flesh and blood women, powerful in their own right, living life on their own terms. What would life have been like if you were an Amazon.

Here are some Amazon names should you want to rename yourself for this exercise: Aella, Derinoe, Antiope, Tecmessa, Polydora, Lomache, Myrto, Hyginus, Lysippe, Gryne, Andro, and Thermodosa.

REWRITE YOUR CREATION STORY:

Journal Page:

Practice

Finally, if you want to write, you have to just shut up, pick up a pen, and do it. I'm sorry there are no true excuses. This is our life. Step forward. Maybe it's only for ten minutes. That's okay. To write feels better than all the excuses.
Natalie Goldberg

Once you find something that calls to you, practice it.

IN THE FOLLOWING chapters, I write about different ways that I express my creativity. I hope one or more of these ways will inspire you.

Once you find something that calls to you, practice it. Try to do it daily or on some kind of schedule that works with your natural rhythms. Make it a part of your life. Make a practice of it. And then practice, practice, practice.

Journaling

We have to dare to be ourselves, however frightening or strange that self may prove to be.
May Sarton

I HAVE KEPT a journal—or a diary—off and on since I was a girl. My parents got me a lined record book for Christmas 1964 when I was nine years old. I wrote on the khaki-colored cover: "Dear Diary," and "Stay-out!"

"12-24-64 Today was Christmas Eve. Work, work, work! First I watched T.V. Then I cleaned my room, boy was that hard." I crossed out the "boy was that hard" part. "My Dad offered to help me. But it ended up I finished it *myself!* . . . After our supper Dad read us a story about a man named Scrooge. It was a Christmas Story. We went to bed, we had a little trouble doing it."

Since I've nearly always thought of myself as a writer, I never had trouble writing in a journal. However, I also always had the sense that someone else would be reading it someday. In other words, I wrote it for an audience—or at least with an audience in mind. When I was younger, that audience was my mother. I knew she read my diary, so I rarely said anything negative about my family. At one point I wrote that my father wouldn't be there for my birth-

> I wrote it for an audience—or at least with an audience in mind.

day and I was disappointed. This probably meant I was *very* upset.

The lack of privacy kept me from expressing my true feelings in my journals. This idea that I was writing for an audience carried over into my adult life.

Although no one was reading my journals after I left home, I was aware that someday someone might, so when I was feeling particularly desperate, depressed, sick, or pissed off, I didn't say so. I will write about my private thoughts and feelings, but they are not my deepest, darkest most personal thoughts and feelings.

So I don't use my journals to vent private thoughts, necessarily, but I do use them as records of my life. These records are very helpful as research tools when I'm writing.

I try to always journal (or blog) when I'm on the road. I record how much things cost, where we stayed, the smells, sights, and rhythms of a place. Later when I want to write about a place I've visited, the journal helps jog my memory.

For instance, I recently wrote an essay about Daphne du Maurier's book *Rebecca*. I met Daphne du Maurier when I was 18 years old and spent some time in her village one summer when I was backpacking across Europe. I reread my journal entries for those days to remind me about the experience. I had forgotten a great deal, and I had remembered some of the experience incorrectly. (I'm assuming my journal entry was more accurate.)

For years, I only wrote in a dead tree journal, not on the computer. But once I got a laptop and started a blog, I most often used the computer—although I still had journals all over the house. For me, my blog was my journal for a long time. I didn't write anything too personal, but I did write about the details of my life.

Sometimes I'll decide to journal for a year, with a theme. Recently I used my *Old Mermaids Book of*

Days and Nights to do a year and a day of living the Old Mermaids Way.

When we moved into town, I decided to walk down to the Columbia River every day and then write about what I saw, experienced, and thought during this daily journey. I called it *River Walk*.

Journals are useful in documenting the changes in the season, too—and on our planet. I find this particularly useful for writing. I can look at my journals for details that I can drop into my stories or essays to make them feel more real—truer.

> And remember, it's for you, not an audience.

CREATIVITY TIP

Decorate this workbook. Put photographs in it. Draw. Write. Make it an expression of you.

And remember, it's for you, not an audience.

Journal Page:

Visual Arts

*If you hear a voice within you say
"you cannot paint," then by all means paint,
and that voice will be silenced.*
Vincent Van Gogh

HOW ABOUT EXERCISING those creative muscles by trying your hand at painting, drawing, or photography? If you're interested in painting, take a class. Or read *Drawing on the Right Side of the Brain* by Betty Edwards. It is the best book on drawing I've ever read. She takes you back to when you were a child and enjoyed drawing, before you got frustrated because your drawings did not turn out exactly the way you expected. After you learn the basics, then you can decide whether you want to pursue it or not.

Here are some visual arts I enjoy.

Collages

When I was a teenager, I started making collages. I ripped out pictures and words that I liked from old magazines, found a big poster board in a color I liked (usually pale blue), arranged the magazine clippings in a way that was pleasing to my eye, and then I glued them onto the poster board. I hung these collages on my bedroom walls where I saw them every day. I liked looking at them. I was meditating on them before I knew what meditation was.

Twenty years later, I attended a week-long workshop and retreat with Vicki Noble and Demetra George on Whidbey Island in Washington. Vicki and Demetra had asked us ahead of time to bring along magazine clippings, poster board, and glue. We spent one of the workshop days doing collages as a group. Each of us created our own collage, but we shared clippings with one another. I remember thinking this was a strange exercise to do. I felt a little foolish. Vicki suggested we think of collages as a kind of visual wish list.

So I did the collage and took it home. Once again I put the collage on my wall where I looked at it every day. I liked seeing the pictures of strong women, delicious-looking food, and a warm and inviting house. I kept it on my wall for a year or so.

Every time I worked with Vicki Noble, we created collages. Often we made them in mandalas, with someone or something representing ourselves at the center. I would then surround the center with colorful pictures representing the directions and elements. Perhaps blue for east, yellow for south, red for west, green for north. Or another time, I might use white for east, red for south, blue for west, black for north.

I now enjoy this process. I like looking for beautiful pictures and then arranging them on a page or a poster board. I have continued this practice with my seven year old neighbor. We'll sit on the floor for hours creating collages. Of course, she does about three collages for every one of mine. Her goal seems to be speed rather than contemplation. But then, she is only seven.

The idea is to create a picture that is pleasing for you to look at. Think of a theme or goal, if you like. Perhaps you want it to be a healing collage. If that's the case, choose images which seem healing to you.

> The idea is to create a picture that is pleasing for you to look at.

If you need prosperity, choose pictures, cards, and items which say prosperity to you.

I recommend trying your hand at putting together a creativity collage. Create something that will pique your creativity every time you look at it. Put together a collage that is beautiful and inspiring.

Forty-six days before my forty-sixth birthday, I started making a collage a day. The first one represented my first year of life. I put a photo of me as an infant at the center. Then I glued pictures around me that represented gifts I wished I had gotten when I was born.

The next day, I did a collage for my second year. And it went on for forty-six days. I made collages for each year of my life: what happened to me during those years, what gifts I wished I'd had during those years, etc. It was a very grounding, meditative experience.

Urban Petroglyphs

I find words around town I like or can "rewrite." Then I take paper and crayons and create what I call "urban petroglyphs." For instance, down by the railroad tracks, the letters OMNI are raised in rubber between the tracks. Since OM is the mother mantra and something I regularly chant, I decided I wanted to create a petroglyph of OM. First I picked a blue-green crayon which I felt was appropriate for OM. Then I put the paper down on the rubber, and I rubbed the crayon over it, until it raised up the letters OM. I was careful not to raise up NI, too. Once I had the raised letters, I continued coloring the rest of the page until I had the effect I wanted.

Drainage covers often have great words. One near my house says "storm." A smaller metal cover had the word WATER and INDIA on it. I used a light blue crayon and raised up WATER and INDIA. When I got home, I got white glue and used it like a pen to write out the word Tara on another sheet of paper.

> I liked seeing the pictures of strong women, delicious-looking food, a warm and inviting house.

(Tara is an Indian goddess often associated with water.) Once the glue had dried, I completed my urban petroglyph by putting the WATER/INDIA paper over the Tara and then rubbing the blue crayon over the glue. It raised right up next to WATER/INDIA. Then I found a frame for the paper and hung it on my wall.

I've done an urban petroglyph of the pattern on my kitchen floor. First I drew a star with white glue, waited until it hardened; then I raised it up using a blue/green crayon. Next I put that paper on the kitchen floor and rubbed until the pattern of the floor was also on the paper. I called the finished product "Falling Star on a Sea-foam Green Kitchen Floor." I framed this and hung it up, too.

Creating urban petroglyphs helps me be more observant of my familiar surroundings.

> Creating the petroglyphs helps me be more observant of my familiar surroundings.

CLAY

Buy yourself some real clay, real Earth, at an art store or from a local potter. You can usually get twenty or thirty pounds of gray or red clay for under ten dollars.

I've never read a word about how to work with clay. I'm sure what I do would make professional potters squirm. I take the clay home and wait for the right moment before I begin. It could be hours or days or weeks. I couldn't even tell you what constitutes the right time. But when that time comes, I turn on music that feels appropriate for my mood. I plop the clay onto a shiny surface, pull off a glob of it, and start to shape it. I go with how I feel.

Recently I used about ten pounds of clay to make a huge snake goddess, her arms straight out, her huge feet anchoring her to the ground, with snakes crawling all over her. Afterward, I sprinkled glitter and stars on her.

One day after going to a waterfall and finding garbage all around it, I came home and created a screaming goddess out of red clay. I put found objects all over her body: pins, toy horses, nails, tiny feathers. All were an expression of my anger over the trashing of the environment.

Some of these clay creations I give away. Others I put outside and let the rain and wind dissolve them: earth to earth again. I equate them with sand paintings. I assume the healing is released as the artwork disappears.

Photography

I have always been interested in photography, but I never pursued it because I knew "real" photographers had to develop their own pictures. I couldn't and wouldn't work with those chemicals, so I rarely picked up a camera. For a time, Mario worked as a professional photographer (although he didn't develop his own photographs), and I often pointed out to him things I thought would make great pictures. I had an idea of what it would look like in my head—or what I wanted it to look like.

Mario encouraged me to get a camera and start taking photographs. I didn't have to be a "great" photographer who developed my own pictures. I could do it my own way. And then, of course, the technology changed. We got an inexpensive scanner and color printer, and suddenly I could take photographs, scan them, and "develop" them into what I wanted.

Mario introduced me to the macro lens, and I was in love. With Mario as my teacher, I started taking close-up photographs of flowers. I wanted to do with photographs what Georgia O'Keeffe had done with paintings. I loved getting so close to the flowers that I could see the veins on the petals. Like the urban petroglyphs, taking photographs made me more observant, steadier in the world.

The thing with photography that is different for me than any other creative work is that I can't control it. At least not yet. I've been writing for so long that I don't try to control the process—I let it flow. But

> When I'm taking photos, I am in the here and now, and it is an extremely relaxing experience for me.

with that experience comes a sense of control, if that makes any sense. With photography, especially using the macro lens, I can't get attached to how each photograph will turn out—because my hands could have been shaking too much, the wind could have shaken the flower too much, or it could be out of focus. I just need to keep taking the photographs.

CREATIVITY TIP

As you may have guessed, this entire chapter is a creative exercise. Pick something you don't normally do and do it. If you write, go paint. If you paint, write. If you usually take photographs, try creating a collage. And you know my mantra: Have fun! Don't worry about perfection.

Journal Page:

Fiction

All you have to do is write one true sentence. Write the truest sentence that you know.
Ernest Hemingway

Fiction is the truth inside the lie.
Stephen King

AS I TOLD you before, I have been writing stories since I was able to write. It is so much a part of who I am it is difficult to pull it apart and see how I do it. It's like eating for me. I just do it.

I don't write every day. Sometimes I don't write for weeks, maybe even months, although that is happening less and less. When I wrote a novel a year and did little or no nonfiction, I could spend a year writing the book or I could spend three months. It all depended upon how much research I had to do and how the actual story flowed. Now I can write a novel in a few weeks if I'm ready. I've opened up that story gate, and it often comes flooding through.

The best thing to do is to find your natural creative rhythm. Mario needs to write nearly every day to stay in his rhythm. I don't. I sometimes need long breaks away from it. I trust the process enough to know I will be able to come back to it when it is time.

Writing for me is almost a compulsion. I have

to do it. When I'm in the midst of a novel, I will think about it all day long as I go about my life. I will dream of it, and I will wake up ready to write. I used to write longhand, 20 to 50 pages a day. Now I write on my laptop.

How do I begin? Ideas come to me. I'll try to remember to write down any thoughts I have on a particular novel and put them in a folder. I'll usually have five to ten novel ideas at a time. Sometimes two ideas will merge into one novel. Eventually, one of these ideas will become prevalent in my thoughts. I'll do research if that's necessary. I'll ruminate on it. Then one day I'll wake up and start writing it.

I get story ideas from everywhere: books, conversations with people, events in my own life. When I was in college, I read a book on writing (I don't remember which one) and the author relayed a supposedly true story about some famous writer. This famous writer and his fellow writers were sitting in a pub drinking. The others were lamenting their paucity of writing ideas. The famous writer said, "I could spend a lifetime writing about the grease spot on the wall behind your head."

I remember thinking, "Yes! Of course!" Think about all the people who sat where the writer was sitting when he made the remark. Think of their lives and the people they knew and the lives of the people they knew—and on and on. Life is a writer's paradise.

For me, writing has always been about communicating to the world—or with the world. I have something to say, something to relate, and I do that better writing a novel than I do sitting around with a group of people talking. "Me" gets out of the way of me when I write. At this stage in my writing life, I feel like the characters come to me and tell me a story, and I'm taking dictation.

For the most part, I don't make detailed outlines. If I did that, I would no longer be interested in writ-

> I don't believe in suffering for my art. I want it to be a joyous process.

ing the book. Although I know the main characters and the plot skeleton ahead of time, I don't want to know everything or I become bored. I usually have an idea of the opening scene, the ending, and what main idea or feeling I would like the readers to take away with them. I know this because the main character has conveyed all of this to me.

Not all my novel ideas become novels. I don't talk about the plots or my ideas ahead of time to anyone. I might bounce an idea off Mario, but I trust him to say only what needs to be said. I don't know of any writers who go around telling the plots of their books to people—there might be some, but I've never met any. Most of the time when someone tells me a plot of a book and claims to be a writer, I know he's not going to write it. In my experience, writers write their stories; they don't talk about them.

The process of creating a story or novel can be a delicate thing. If you tell someone what you're doing, and they say the wrong thing, you might become discouraged and not write the novel. When I had an agent, that sometimes happened to me. I would briefly tell him what I was interested in writing, and if he didn't sound excited, I lost interest.

Writing requires a great deal of energy and concentration. I have to be careful that I eat well, have a good sleep schedule, and exercise enough. When I'm in the throes of novel writing, that is all I want to do. Everything else seems superfluous.

When I finish a novel, I usually read it to Mario. Then I go through it once and make corrections. After that, I put it away for a time. When I'm ready, I'll bring it out. Mario and I will both read it, and I'll make changes where necessary.

I don't do a lot of major revisions any more. If the novel is so bad that I have to do too much, I'll junk the book and figure that's a lesson learned. Some people can rewrite and rewrite and rewrite. Personally, I don't like to read books that have been rewrit-

> I don't think about audience. I don't think about whether I can sell it to a publisher. I don't think. I listen and I write.

ten within an inch of their lives, so to speak. Something happens in those books, something is lost—the magic is gone. Spent.

But that's me.

I write quickly for the most part. I don't believe in suffering for my art. I want it to be a joyous process. If I'm not able to write quickly on a novel, it often means I'm not ready to write it. Or it could mean it's not a workable idea. But that's not true for everyone. I have been writing for a very long time—since I was five years old. That means I've been doing it for five decades at this point. With experience, I've gained the ability to write quickly. I'm able to let go and let it flow.

I agree with every writing instructor out there who says a writer should read, read, read. I would add that you should write, write, write, too. And, most of all, try to live a life of joy. The idea that one has to suffer to be an artist is nonsense. You will suffer, you will have difficult times, but that's life. Turn it around to your advantage and write about it.

The modern maxim "do what you love and the money will follow" is also nonsense. You should do what you love, but the money may or may not follow.

The best book I've read about writing short fiction is Damon Knight's *Creating Short Fiction. On Becoming a Novelist* by John Gardner is the best book about writing novels I've ever read.

Wait. I have just told you about all of the practicalities of writing, haven't I? But that's not the entire story.

This is how I write fiction now: A character comes up to me (knocks on the door to my imagination) and tells me her story. I write down what she tells me.

My job—or my talent—is to turn this tale into something coherent and beautiful. After that, my job is to get this character's story out into the world.

As I mentioned, I write quickly now, but that wasn't always the way. For a long time, I wrote a

> Most of all, try to live a life of joy.

novel a year, and the process could sometimes be tedious. I was so glad when I started writing more quickly. This change in my process began a few years ago when a young girl named Mercy began telling me her story. Her story became the book *Mercy, Unbound*.

By the way, I don't think about audience when I write. I don't think about whether I can sell it to a publisher or to a reader. I don't think. I listen and I write.

I go with the flow.

Go with the flow.

Sometimes it's difficult. For instance, I don't like it when characters talk to me in a dialect. It's difficult to transcribe. Ruby had her own way of speaking, and I wrote it down. (This book became *Ruby's Imagine*.) After I finished, I had to edit the book, but Ruby had told me her story, and now her voice was gone. My publisher's copyeditor wanted to change many, many things to make Ruby's dialect more consistent. I had to trust what Ruby had told me in the first place, so I didn't let her change a word. That was scary, but I'm glad I did it. Ruby's story is probably the most beautiful story I've ever been privileged to write.

One day an Irish woman came to me and told me her story. I wrote it down, and it became the novel *The Fish Wife*. When I read the book, I hear her Irish accent, but I don't know if anyone else does.

Once a Pakistani girl wanted me to tell her story. That was terrifying. I knew nothing about being a Pakistani girl. In the end, I had to listen and write down that story which became the novel *Broken Moon*. I did research to fill in any blanks.

This was true for *Ruby's Imagine,* too. I researched what happened before, during, and after Hurricane Katrina for about a year before and during the writing of that book.

I go to Arizona for a month every year to write. During that month, I almost always write a novel. One year I wrote two. The first book I wrote there was *Church of the Old Mermaids*. I sat in a tiny house in the desert, and thirteen Old Mermaids stepped out of the Old Sea and into the wash that ran in front of this little house—the Quail House—and they told me their stories. And I wrote them down.

I am still writing down Old Mermaid stories, and I love them.

So do your work. Learn your skills. Practice, practice, practice. And let your imagination go. Don't bridle it. Don't harness it. Creativity isn't a horse race where we're all running around in a circle on a dirt track, all looking alike, all running alike. Creativity is more like a wild horse running across the plains, free and part of nature.

Creativity is about going with the flow. It is about being filled up with your true self—being full of yourself—and letting your natural creative tendencies flow.

Yes. This is what I have found to be true.

> Creativity is more like a wild horse running across the plains, free and part of nature.

CREATIVITY TIP

Set a goal for yourself. You figure out what kind of goal works best: Is it daily, weekly, monthly, yearly? My husband writes for about an hour before work, five days a week. He writes at least 1,000 words at each of these sittings. This means he writes about 250,000 words a year; that's the equivalent of at least three books a year. He does this one day at a time. He calls it his writing practice. (More on this later.) If you're not a writer, you come up with your own practice: paint, dance, cook, draw, or play music for an hour a day. Or three hours a day. You decide.

Lately, like Mario, I've been writing at least 1,000 words a day, five days a week. We don't beat up on ourselves if we miss a day. We just start again the next day. The purpose of a goal and/or a practice is to encourage ourselves and give our creative muscles a workout so that each time it gets a little easier and feels a little more natural.

Goal:

Journal Page:

Creative Nonfiction

*We write to taste life twice,
in the moment and in retrospect.*
Anaïs Nin

I DIDN'T WRITE nonfiction for most of my life, except for high school and college essays. When I was older, I wanted to write nonfiction, especially about Nature, but I would read other writers and know I could never write like Terry Tempest Williams or David Abram or Susan Griffith. I was completely intimidated.

But I got older and braver, I suppose. I published a fiction magazine for a while and wrote editorials for each issue. I published a tiny Nature magazine, and most of it contained my essays about surviving and thriving in this old world.

I started writing short essays after trips into the woods. As I explored Nature, I wrote about it and my feelings about what I was experiencing.

What helped me to write nonfiction was to sit down and write it. I started a blog and wrote on it often. That loosened up my nonfiction muscles. Writing on the blog helped me get over my desire to be

> The best art, the best piece of writing, often reveals just as much about the artist as it does about the world.

perfect. I was writing quickly, and I was writing every day. So naturally, every word was not perfect. After a while, I began writing political essays during the war with Iraq, and I sold quite a few to online publishers.

Creative nonfiction is still not as easy for me as fiction writing. I do my best work when I relate the topic to myself and my world. Although I was a journalist when I was in college, I excelled as a feature writer rather than a straight news reporter. I liked the creative part better than the "just the facts, ma'am" part of news reporting.

For me, the best nonfiction reveals something unknown or unseen. This is sometimes best done by revealing ourselves. The best art, the best piece of writing, often reveals as much about the artist as it does about the world. The art of it all is in the balance—in telling just enough about ourselves to lead the reader or the viewer into the other place, the other world you are discussing in your essay.

Below you will find one of my recent essays which I hope demonstrates what I am talking about.

Essay: Sea Women

I write about mermaids. Not little mermaids. Not those over-sexed depictions of mermaids we see everywhere, with their breasts pointing to the sky and their backs arched like some kind of wannabe Playboy mer-bunny. No. My mermaids are old mermaids. Ancient. They are creators and destroyers, poets and dreamers, artists and musicians, cooks and gardeners, mystics and conjurers, leaders and mediators, witches and sorcerers. They are sirens, calling us to our true wild selves. They are oceanic and powerful, not mere maids, but goddesses all.

I came to mermaids not as a child but as a grown woman. As a young girl, I wasn't interested in anything frilly or girlie. At least not that I can remember. I played with trains and printing presses. I wrote stories and books and created an imaginary world where girls and women ruled and had magical powers. Any depictions I saw of mermaids made me think they were powerless, so I wasn't interested.

Later as an adult, I studied goddess mythology and came across fish-tailed goddesses, but I didn't relate them to the European stories of mermaids who supposedly lured men to their deaths. Then one winter, I was sitting at my annual writing retreat in Arizona when thirteen women calling themselves Old Mermaids walked out of the Old Sea and into my life. They begin whispering stories to me, so I began writing the novel *Church of the Old Mermaids*.

I was baffled but interested when these mermaids appeared in my imagination, so I started doing research on mermaids. I learned that one of the first depictions of a goddess was the Syrian fish-goddess Atargatis (who was also known later as Aphrodite). In fact, many cultures had stories of ancient fish-tailed goddesses and myths and legends of mermaid-like creatures belonging to seas, oceans, and lakes. It seemed the modern mermaid was a transformation of the ancient goddess from a powerful creatrix of all life to a kind of fish-tailed Barbie.

During this time, I saw a painting of Yemaya rising out of the ocean—her skin black and her tail bright blue—and I was filled with awe. I could almost hear her head breaking the surface of the water as she rose, could almost feel the drops of ocean and sense the sea shiver as she made Herself visible. I understood then, fully, the power of the symbol of woman as part fish. She was the ocean and she was woman. She was all powerful—the birthplace of life.

Mermaids are ubiquitous these days. Young adult novels are swimming with mermaids. Depictions of them are all over the internet. Is this commercialization of mermaids watering down their power? Or have their powers already diminished over time? After all, most of us have either forgotten or never

> My mermaids are old mermaids. Ancient. They are creators and destroyers, poets and dreamers, artists and musicians, cooks and gardeners, mystics and conjurers, leaders and mediators, witches and sorcerers.

knew their genesis as fish-tailed goddesses of birth and death.

My 7-year-old neighbor likes mermaids. The other day she brought over one of her favorite books about a Barbie mermaid, along with several small Barbie-like mermaid dolls. They looked alike, all very thin with bigger breasts than a real woman that thin would actually have. Nothing powerful or goddess-like about these creatures. They struck me as the latest doll form of woman as a kind of monoculture.

Despite the Barbie-ization of mermaids, I wondered why these particular mythological creatures had suddenly become so popular. Was it a whim of culture or some form of commercialization?

Then why did they come to *me* eight winters ago, before this present mermaid craze? They came into my imagination and I wrote about them. And I keep writing about them. I had never written about the same characters or the same world before. Since *Church of the Old Mermaids,* I wrote a kind of prequel to it, *The Fish Wife.* And the Old Mermaids are supporting characters in *The Desert Siren* and *The Blue Tail.* I've put together a book of quotes (mostly culled from the Old Mermaids books) called *The Old Mermaids Book of Days and Nights.* And I have many other Old Mermaids novels in mind.

> I believe storytellers are voices for the planet.

Why now? Mermaids come from the watery realms. Carl Jung and others might say they represent the feminine—maybe even the submerged feminine. Perhaps it's more literal than that. Could it be they've stepped out of the Imaginal Realms to remind us that we are the blue planet, the water planet, and our waterways are in trouble? Without clean oceans and rivers, we die, along with most other creatures on this planet. As climate change wreaks havoc on our weather systems and drives water temperatures dangerously high, is it any wonder that a creature from the watery depths rises up and cries, "Answer the call to the wild! It is time. Wake up, now. Wake up!"

Where I live in the Pacific Northwest, Sasquatch is part of the local legends. You don't have to go far before you find someone who has a story about seeing or almost seeing Bigfoot. But according to some Native American beliefs, Sasquatch only shows up when life is out of balance: You do not want to see a Bigfoot because it means things are either not going well or bad things are about to happen.

Maybe mermaids—in my case, Old Mermaids—are appearing to warn us or to show us that life is out of balance.

I know that sounds like a stretch. One could ask, why are vampires so popular then? What message from the collective psyche do they bring? I really don't know. But I do believe stories are important. I believe storytellers are voices for the planet: We speak for the planet and all her creatures. Some stories—maybe all?—come to us from the Imaginal Realms for some reason: to teach, enlighten, warn, encourage.

When I was 19 years old, I tried to kill myself. I didn't want to die, but I wanted the awful emotional pain to stop. Afterward, I moved out of the house I shared with three other women and into a tiny attic apartment. For weeks (maybe even a year), I barely said a word to anyone—beyond what was necessary to get through the day since I was working and going to school full-time. One night I dreamed about a water nymph. I remember thinking she was a naiad even though I didn't actually know what a naiad was. She had water and seaweed running up and down her very white body. She had big soulful eyes. In the dream, we made love all night long. It was a profound healing. When I awoke the next morning, I began to recover and I knew I would survive. Years later, I realized she was probably my first encounter with the Old Mermaids.

Mermaids next appeared to me eight winters ago, just two months before I had two surgeries—that was

> Some stories—maybe all?—come to us from the Imaginal Realms for some reason: to teach, enlighten, warn, encourage.

> I hope we can finally and forever be full of our powerful true wild oceanic selves

when I wrote *Church of the Old Mermaids*—and they haven't left me since. Their appearance in my life has felt extraordinary.

Can they be more than that? Are their appearances or re-appearances on this planet a siren call to us all? Can the stories about them be more than escapist fiction? Can the mermaids—and Old Mermaids in particular—help us uncover or compose our own siren songs—that part of us that is true and valiant and able?

I hope so. I hope we can finally and forever be full of our powerful true wild oceanic selves—we can be sea women and men—ready to ride the waves of our lives and fix that which is broken and heal that which is sick.

After all, we are creators and destroyers, poets and dreamers, artists and musicians, cooks and gardeners, mystics and conjurers, leaders and mediators, witches and sorcerers. It is time to awaken and heal ourselves and the world.

Creativity Tip

You've entered the discomfort zone.

Step out of your comfort zone. If writing fiction is easy for you, but you're feeling dissatisfied, do something else. Draw a picture, take a photograph, write an article. If you're a painter, write something. Do something creatively that makes you uncomfortable. This helps nudge your brain and imagination out of any ruts.

You don't have to do it for long or forever. Just do it. And don't judge. Whenever I draw, I get frustrated because it doesn't turn out exactly the way I expected. Years later, I'll look at something I've drawn and I'll think, "What was I fussing about? I like this."

My stories never turn out exactly like I imagine they will, and yet I'm fine with that because I trust that particular process. I need to learn to trust the process when I create visual art, too. That's the key to so much of creativity: learning to trust yourself.

STEP INTO YOUR DISCOMFORT ZONE:

JOURNAL PAGE:

Poetry

by Mario Milosevic

*If I feel physically as if the top of my head
were taken off, I know that is poetry.*
Emily Dickinson

ALL OF THE best creativity advice I've ever heard can be boiled down to one sentence: *Get out of your own way and do the work.*

That's it.

There are many variations of this.

The artist Frederick Franck has 10 commandments for drawing. Here's number 2: *You shall not wait for inspiration, for it comes not while you wait but while you work.*

Jane Yolen advocates a method of writing she calls BIC: *Butt In Chair.*

William Faulkner said something like this: *I only write when I am inspired. Fortunately I am inspired every day at nine a.m.*

Tina Fey says: *You don't go on because it's ready. You go on because it's 11:30.*

Here's Robert Heinlein's five rules for writing:

1. You must write.

2. You must finish what you write.

> The best thing for your creative well-being, always, is to do the next project.

3. You must not rewrite except to editorial request.

4. You must put it on the market.

5. You must keep it on the market until sold.

All of these practitioners of the creative arts, and many more besides, learned the most important lesson of creativity and then applied it: persevere. When in doubt, paint another picture, write another poem, shape another sculpture, compose another song, or film another movie.

It's really that simple.

Don't worry about perfection. Just do the work. Or, if that sounds too much like drudgery, do the play.

Whatever you call it, revel in your creative juices. Don't try to stifle yourself or tell yourself it's not as good as you hoped it would be or it's not as good as someone else's work or if you spent a little more time *tweaking* it you will get it right.

Don't worry that there have been millions of novels and songs written before yours. None of them will be *your* song. None of those novels will have *your* sensibility.

The best thing for your creative well-being, always, is to do the next project.

Take your lesson from nature. She doesn't spend years perfecting one tree. No. She sends out hundreds, even *thousands*, of seeds from even the most modest of plants. Most of those seeds will simply fade away. But some of them will take root, become beautiful flowers, or incredibly strong and long-lived trees, or amazingly sturdy weeds, the stout rascals of the plant world.

Who are you to argue with nature's methods, surely the most creative force in the universe? Study her and you will see your path forward: create and release. Then repeat. Again and again.

If you doubt me, try it for a short time and see what happens to your creative soul and spirit. Expand your practice. Nurture fecundity. Make a draw-

Take your lesson from nature.

ing a day for a month. Write a short story a week for a season.

My revelation came when I decided to write a poem a day for a year.

Understand that I had written perhaps two or three poems up to that time. Poetry was not part of my world. I was a short story writer and a novelist.

But I had not yet learned the power of perseverance, and my production had dropped to a trickle. I wanted to write, desperately, but I was concerned that I didn't know enough, that I wasn't good enough, and that most of what I produced was sub par.

All of this was terrible for the creative impulse within me.

Kim noticed that I was producing very little work and suggested that I might not be a writer anymore.

We've all heard of wake-up calls. That was a wake-up call for me. It galvanized me into reconsidering my creative life. Was I a writer? Well, if the definition of writer is someone who writes, then, no, I wasn't much of one at that time.

And yet, even knowing that did not help. I was not immediately motivated to take up the pen and boldly jump into my next novel. It only made me feel more down about myself.

What I did instead was cast about for a different means of expression. Something new and challenging. What I settled on was poetry, an unknown country for me. What I decided was I would learn how to write poems.

Where that idea came from, I still—to this day—don't know. Why didn't I decide to try creative nonfiction, or jump out of writing completely and take up watercolor or compose music instead? I don't know. The ways of the creative spirit are mysterious and not always subject to analysis. It might even be best to refrain from analyzing such things. Dissection, after all, usually kills the subject.

> Let's just say the poetic muse nudged me and leave it at that.

Let's just say the poetic muse nudged me and leave it at that.

I quickly evolved a practice for my project. Most days I woke up early, leaving myself a good hour before I had to get ready for work.

The time constraint was probably very helpful here. I had to come up with something in that hour.

Most days I wrote down a first line at random. That line suggested another, and then another, and so on.

I didn't work completely blind. I found books on poetry that explained all the different forms: sonnets, limericks, sestinas, blank verse, tritinas, and so on. There are many forms of poetry, a seemingly endless garden of them. I tried my hand at many of them, working the fertile soil of verse, rhymes, and metrical composition.

Far from being a constraint, for me, the rules and conventions of formal poetry felt like a stage. They allowed me freedom of expression within the confines of a sturdy platform and wondrous props.

I didn't care if my sonnets were not as good as Shakespeare's or if my villanelles fell flat. None of that mattered. What mattered is that I was doing the work.

I read other poets and found wonderful things to appreciate in their work. But mostly I wrote my own.

Some mornings I would arrive at my writing desk with nothing. No idea, no inspiration. That didn't stop me. I made myself have an idea and wrote the poem. Sometimes the resulting poems were successful, and sometimes they weren't.

But that didn't matter. Remember the plants sending out all those seeds? Not every seed is perfect. I didn't need every one of my poems to be perfect.

Another thing I discovered was that by working every day, I was in the best position to take advantage of inspiration when it did come. I never would have thought, before I started my daily practice, that

> Not every seed is perfect. I didn't need every one of my poems to be perfect.

I would write a poem about baseball. But one morning, casting about for a subject for my daily poem, I recalled a game I played when I was nine years old. The habit of poem writing I had developed allowed me to take this fleeting image and turn it into a poem.

That wouldn't have happened, *couldn't* have happened, if I had not developed my practice over the preceding months.

I completed my project successfully. I went a whole year of writing poems without missing a single day. At the end, I was still so happy with what I was doing that I continued without a break. I ended up going three full years of writing a poem a day.

Some days I wrote more than one poem. I would write one in the morning, then, still brimming with creative ideas, I would write another one in the evening. I recall a few days when I did three or four.

But those were rare. My practice was a poem a day and I stuck to that.

During those three years I began sending out my poems to magazines and anthologies. The vast majority of them came back. This did not bother me. Nature is not bothered by the seeds that do not germinate.

Soon enough, some of my poems found receptive editors who liked what I was doing and included my poems in their publications. This was gratifying. I loved every acceptance, but the true work, the work that mattered, was still at the keyboard, writing my poem a day.

It wouldn't have mattered if no editor ever bought a single poem of mine. What mattered was the doing. The practice.

I ended up writing approximately 1200 poems over those three years and placing about 110 of them in various publications. I've collected many of my favorites into three books of poetry: *Animal Life, Fantasy Life,* and *Love Life.*

> By working every day, I was in the best position to take advantage of inspiration when it did come.

All of the poems in those books were written in one day.

My career as a poet was short-lived. After my three years of writing a poem a day, I returned to prose with renewed vigor. I began producing short stories and novels at a quicker pace, with more confidence.

I still struggle with doubts about my talent and ability. Many creative people do. But what I learned from my poetry project was that it is always a good idea to do the next project. Always.

Doing the next project keeps you in the creative mode. It keeps the synapses firing and makes connections you couldn't or wouldn't have made otherwise.

Perseverance and fecundity.

Be prolific. It's the best way to get better and have fun.

> What mattered was the doing. The practice.

CREATIVITY TIP

Kim here again:

Write anywhere. Draw anywhere. Dance everywhere. Although it's nice to have a room of one's own, so to speak, don't be tied to it. Don't fall into the trap of "I'll write when I get settled," "I'll paint when I feel better," "I'll play when I'm happy," "I'll create when I have my own room." Let creation be like breathing: natural. When I was in college in Ypsilanti, Michigan, I used to drive to the Renaissance Center in Detroit. I'd go into the busiest, noisiest part of it, find a place to sit, and I'd write. I wanted to train myself to be able to write anywhere and anytime. And it pretty much worked. I highly recommend it.

WRITE ANYWHERE ANYTIME:

Journal Page:

Be Full of Yourself

*One day I will find the right words,
and they will be simple.*
Jack Kerouac

YOU'VE HEARD FROM Mario Milosevic, and you've heard from me.

I could go on, but I think you get the idea. You can be creative in how you dress, how you cook, how you live your life, how you raise your children, how you participate in your community, and how you love your sweetheart. Every act in our lives is essentially a creative act, isn't it?

Or could be.

So be yourself. Don't try to be like anyone else. Don't denigrate your work. Don't be overly critical of your work. In fact, while you are creating, don't be critical at all. Later, you will need your critical eye. But remember that critical eye is never cruel or belittling: It is inspiring.

Have fun. Remember to dance, love, play, laugh, giggle, and plan creative revolutions. Creativity is at the heart of everything—especially at the heart of you.

> Creativity is at the heart of everything—especially at the heart of you.

About the Author

KIM ANTIEAU PRACTICES the creative life. She writes, gardens, sculpts, takes photographs, and helps create public art. Her books include *The Monster's Daughter, Under the Tucson Moon, Church of the Old Mermaids, The Jigsaw Woman, Ruby's Imagine, Fun with Vic and Jane,* and many more. She is creative director of *The Wayward Arts* and creator of *We Are Here: Geography of the Heart.* Kim teaches *The Old Mermaids Mystery School* and *The Old Mermaids School of Everything.* She lives with her husband, writer Mario Milosevic. Learn more at www.kimantieau.com.

www.ingramcontent.com/pod-product-compliance
Lightning Source LLC
Chambersburg PA
CBHW081721100526
44591CB00016B/2451